D0128472

FRONTIERS OF ACCESS TO LIBRARY MATERIALS
No. 4

DATE DUE

HIGHSMITH   #45102

FRONTIERS OF ACCESS TO LIBRARY MATERIALS

Sheila S. Intner, Series Editor

Budgeting *for* Information Access

Murray S. Martin
Milton T. Wolf

Managing
the Resource
Budget
for Absolute
Access

American Library Association
Chicago and London
1998

While extensive effort has gone into ensuring the reliability of information appearing in this book, the publisher makes no warranty, express or implied, on the accuracy or reliability of the information, and does not assume and hereby disclaims any liability to any person for any loss or damage caused by errors or omissions in this publication.

Project editor: Louise D. Howe

Composition in Caslon and Avant Garde using Xyvision by the dotted i

Printed on 50-pound White Offset, a pH-neutral stock, and bound in 10-point coated cover stock by Data Reproductions

The paper used in this publication meets the minimum requirements of American National Standard for Information Sciences—Permanence of Paper for Printed Library Materials, ANSI Z39.48-1992.♾

Library of Congress Cataloging-in-Publication Data

Martin, Murray S.
    Budgeting for information access : managing the resource budget for absolute access / Murray S. Martin and Milton T. Wolf.
        p.   cm. — (Frontiers of access to library materials ; no. 4)
    Includes bibliographical references (p.   ) and index.
    ISBN 0-8389-0691-5 (alk. paper)
    1. Library materials budgets—United States. 2. Document delivery—United States—Finance. I. Wolf, Milton T. II. Title.
III. Series.
Z689.5.U6M368   1998
025.2'1'0681—dc21   98-10964

Printed in the United States of America.

02 01 00 99 98   5 4 3 2 1

Contents

1
Introduction

The library literature is full of statements about the benefits of considering access in place of, or in addition to, ownership in developing library budgets for resources and services. However, little attention has been paid to the roles *each* must play in the future of libraries, since there is no way of separating the two modes of information access. Even less attention has been paid to how to reach that desirable balance and how to pay for it.

To support such a change, it is necessary to develop institutional mission and goal statements, library mission and goal statements, and a collection development policy that reflects those statements, along with specific ways of handling it. Further, there is a need to define properly what such services as document delivery mean for users and how they will be handled and funded. Also, cooperative resource sharing needs planning and careful implementation—not to mention supportive budgeting. Unless these steps are taken, the potential success of any shift from ownership to access will be in jeopardy. A good examination of some of the issues involved can be found in Intner, where she presents the results of a survey of collection development decision making.[1] A full treatment of the differences can be found in *Access versus Assets,* by Barbra Buckner Higginbotham and Sally Bowdoin,[2] which looks in detail at the role each must play and provides examples of the ways in which libraries have responded to this shift, with particular attention to resource sharing. Despite some apparent claims, resource sharing is not without cost and must be balanced against alternative ways of attaining the same goals.

For instance, one must consider the total effect of relying on external services to supply needed materials and decide whether such a move is actually consistent with the library's priorities. "Access" can mean merely access to bibliographic records, in which case further action is still necessary to retrieve the wanted materials, and is likely to incur further costs. It can also mean access to the materials themselves, most likely in electronic format (many of which are proprietary and costly), in which case there is still a need to print or download the information for use by an individual or by the community at large.

Access can also mean the ability to use the resources of other libraries, whether by a shared library card for borrowing or simply use on the spot. These kinds of settings remind us that there is a significant difference between personal and community benefit, which needs to be looked at in regard to library finance. As Eugene Wiemers explains, we need to mesh thinking about the library marketplace, the actual financial setting, our perception of where we belong, and the actual needs of our users.[3] This topic will be explored more extensively in later chapters, but the notion of user responsiveness is basic to the future of libraries.

All these possibilities for borrowing and access raise a wide range of budgetary issues. Questions that need to be answered include:

- How can either of these procedures (lending and access) be carried out?
- What are the associated costs?
- How do these costs compare with the cost of providing local ownership?

On a different scale, access can also mean providing information to remote users within the institution—internal document delivery—or delivery to other campuses or sites, for example in distance learning. When this is the case one should ask:

- What kinds of effects do these decisions have on the distribution of the library budget?
- Have these effects been adequately considered in making decisions about access?
- Are there any legal considerations?
- What are the effects of an ongoing computerized infrastructure?

This book will try to answer some of these questions or, at least, to provide a framework for better financial decision making. Among the issues that have to be understood are the places to be filled by:

materials

access

maintenance

preservation

equipment

storage

Some of these may not seem primarily resource concerns, but all impact on the ability of the library to deliver information and must be taken into account when planning the budget. Too often in the past, libraries have neglected such secondary budget considerations, only to be brought up short when, for example, an extension or rebuilding of the library is necessary to house added resources, or when it is necessary to rewire the whole building to support electronic access both to the catalog and to outside sources. These situations exemplify the problems faced by any library in the electronic age. They also suggest that there are added financial problems that have, so far, been overlooked.

Budget or Collection Limitations

Libraries have always recognized that their users will want materials they do not own and that, as a result, someone will have to pay for unowned materials, whether by personal purchase; through interlibrary loan, photocopy, or document delivery; or by library purchase in those cases where the need appears to be in line with the library's collection goals. These instances are, however, the result of having already made a conscious policy decision that certain kinds of materials will not be purchased and owned by the library. In all this, the user must be an active partner, otherwise the fundamental collecting decisions made may lead to the library's impoverishment rather than its improvement. Collecting, after all, is for the user, not for the library. As Elaine Goleski says, "What the for-profits can show us at this point is that, if you don't check your view of what the customers want, you may end up producing the Edsel or the New Coke."[4]

Ownership or Access: Budget Implications

What are the budget implications for libraries in deciding what will be "owned," and what "accessed"? Ownership and access have different financial implications. In the first instance (ownership), although the library may undertake certain kinds of expenditures (shelving, repair, and other preservation actions, for example) to ensure that resources are available locally, there is still the issue of how much such a decision costs in terms of staff, processing, and building costs, and what the relation of these costs is to the value of the use made of the materials. In the second (access), these become costs relating to access tools, which are also a collection element, staff, and retrieval—and the library has gained no permanent capital investment from the transaction. Here again, there is the question of user needs, in this case often the need for further education in what is available electronically, and how to access and use it.

Direct comparisons are seldom made between these two sets of costs, nor between the resulting benefits. Studies tend to be of one activity or the other without drawing comparisons, and thus are not of great assistance in planning new budgets. Libraries need to accumulate many more studies of the relationship between collecting materials and serving their users.

Collection Models

These two models (access and ownership) are not exclusive, in the sense that no library has ever been able to own everything that its users may want, but, when push comes to shove, it is essential to determine what proportion of the responses to users' needs for materials can be assigned to ownership or access. The costs of either option vary, so libraries have to decide how to spread the available budget to achieve optimal returns. If the goal is to ensure that library users optimize their use of resources, the library must plan how to develop the best possible response to user needs, as distinct from trying to follow some externally determined budget distribution.[5]

What Is Collection Management?

Adding to resources

Planned deselection (weeding)

Providing access

Maintaining resources

Building connections

Preserving resources

Sharing resources

Discovering the appropriate response is, at best, a problematic endeavor, so variable are the needs relating to the achievement of an appropriate library plan. In an academic library repetitive needs, such as those for course reserve reading, are greatly different from those for a specific research project, and both intermingle with the ongoing needs for teaching, the initial introduction to a subject for graduate students, and general research. The crossover nature of the various needs makes it difficult for the library to assign costs to individual programs or to classes of users.

Special libraries may appear to have their materials needs predefined by the scope of the enterprise—law, accounting, business—but they also have to be aware that these interests may change, particularly in a research enterprise, and all will find an increasing interest in electronic information. In fact, many special libraries have been converted almost totally to electronic format. This is particularly true for legal libraries, where the almost omnipresent Westlaw library services have coasted over the whole issue of whether they can indeed claim copyright protection for their products. The future promises a rather more open field.

In a public library there is continuing need for a wide range of general reading, research support may be needed as much by school children as by adults, and there may be specific business needs to consider. There is also the need to respond to the varying reading levels of children and young people, and, in a different sort of approach, to respond to changes in governmental styles. The need to address different reader audiences—for example, the speech and hearing impaired—has also spurred the public library to diversify its collecting in ways not yet common in other kinds of libraries.

The dynamic nature of libraries is itself a continuing cause of self-reexamination. Too often, either ownership or access is considered without close reference to user needs. User reaction to such unilateral decision making can be quite strong.[6] The idea of restricted access is explored in Isaac Asimov's *Forward the Foundation* (New York: Doubleday, 1993) in which the Librarian of the Galactic Library, faced with severe budget cuts, proposes to make all access available only through the library staff. Although this refers, strictly speaking, to closed stacks, it raises the same kinds of issues and suggests that user needs must be kept in mind whenever decisions are made. If such considerations can appear in science fiction, librarians must be wary of making real a less than desirable future, especially one that crosses into the digital future. This may seem distant, but many information providers are looking to a nonprint future.

Electronic Publishing

The process has been complicated by the emergence of electronic publishing in its various forms: CD-ROMs, databases, either internal or external, or materials available only via Internet or similar networks. Each of these categories of library materials operates under different financial rules. CD-ROMs are purchased, but there may be restrictions on their use. Moreover, if they cover a rapidly changing field, they can go out of date very quickly. In many instances they then become a kind of serial with the difference that each replacement is cumulative. Internal databases (the most common is the online catalog, though we do not generally think of the catalog as a publication) need upkeep, equipment replacement, and staff time. External (off-site) databases are subject to contract law, and their lease by a library or group of libraries has to be negotiated. Simple access may be subject to a variety of charges or restrictions. Again they require equipment, supplies, and staff assistance in their use, not to mention the space, especially the related workstations. Online publications present an entire other range of possibilities. Some are freely accessible, some are available only by subscription, some can be downloaded, some cannot. Be aware also that only too many Web pages are poorly maintained, out of date, and possibly sources for misinformation rather than information.

It is not yet clear what kinds of charges commercial online publishers will levy, but there is a distinct possibility that even access for browsing purposes will bear a charge.[7] These problems arise from the nature of online publishing, where there is less publisher control, and it may well be possible that libraries will have to act as agents for their users. These issues are still in flux, but librarians must continue to be aware of their possible effects on library use of information.

Price Increases

Further, price escalation for serials, especially in scientific and technical fields, has forced libraries to cancel subscriptions and rely on alternative ways of recovery. Some of these will be discussed in later chapters, notably the consortial acquisition of online serials. The most recent price forecasts by serial vendors note that increasing numbers of cancellations have affected the cost of those serials to the remaining subscribers, a sort of secondary price increase spiral. Even with these cancellations, the cost of the retained subscriptions tends to depress expenditures on other media, many of which are not so amenable to the access mode. The annual projections of subscription prices make it clear that annual increases on the order of 10 percent can be expected, a prospect that will surely crunch library acquisitions yet further. It has even been suggested that the age of the serial may be passing, at least in the case of the highly priced journal of record.[8] Attaining this end requires a great deal of cooperation between providers, intermediaries, and consumers. To date, there has been little progress in such consultation.

Budget Responses

In this setting, it is clear that all libraries will have to make decisions each year about how to split up their budgets to obtain needed information by means of an appropriate mix of methods. Although the program or performance budget models that have emerged can give some guidance and, where they are already in place, can be remodeled, the closest budget styles to the new need are transactional budgets, or materials and information handling budgets. These are commercial or industrial styles designed to follow the flow of a product but they can readily be used to determine the costs and benefits of alternative methods of providing information. In addition, they have the side effect of being suited to show the value-added aspect of library activities.

Collection Management Principles

There are two ways of looking at collection management. The first is based on policy, the second on practicality.

The Three Ms

Mission

Money

Motivation

The Three Ps

People

Policies

Programs

These help determine what the library should do, and what it can do, the latter because of budget and staff limitations. These are not simply arbitrary categories, they are the day-to-day components of all library operations and must be taken into account when planning future strategies.

Without following such a methodology it is virtually impossible to determine the most efficacious mix of materials and services. Admittedly, there is no readily identifiable product that has a cost and shows a profit (other than user satisfaction), profit being the prime evaluatory tool in business and industry. There are some possible measures such as the books and other information supplied to meet a need,[9] and the possibility of using supply and demand as appropriate measures for investment. What Herb White wrote many years ago of special libraries applies to *all* libraries, namely, that there is a need to demonstrate cost-effectiveness and cost-benefit. "Librarians have continued, for far too long, to perform their jobs in a traditional way. . . . Libraries, unable to demonstrate their specific contributions to this year's profit growth, have tended to avoid financial analyses altogether."[10]

There is a compelling need for management to be shown that there is some kind of cost-benefit relationship, even if it is difficult to demonstrate in an accounting sense, to justify the existence of the library. The value of reading is only now becoming a prime factor in the information age, since it makes it possible for the users of electronic information to make more informed choices and enables user and provider to communicate at a more productive level. This value-added activity remains the core justification for libraries and their services.

Costs and Benefits

The demonstration of benefits is a somewhat uncharted area in public service and nonprofit accounting, yet it is the inevitable outcome of the use of input/output measures. For too long, libraries, accrediting agencies, states, and other governing bodies have relied heavily on input measures—so many books, so many staff, so much operating expenditure—as evaluative tools. Program and performance budgets have helped in moving the emphasis to output measures—so many books circulated, so many reference questions answered—but they have not often begun with the outputs to determine whether these show an active library. They have started, rather, with the present budget and proposed changes. This may be reasonable in a public finance mode, but does not address the issue of whether these are the most appropriate ways of meeting public demand.

The zero-based budget was supposed to remedy this problem but has, in general, proved too cumbersome for total application, largely because public missions do not differ markedly from year to year. Other factors, such as union contracts or tenure, or the delays inherent in subscription cancellations and the order process generally, have limited its usefulness within the library community. Moreover, the heavy capital investment represented by the library implies relatively slow change, since much library expenditure has to be seen as "value maintenance" of that capital asset.[11] Unless librarians understand this need and can persuade their financing agency of this need, they will undoubtedly fail in the battle for financial support.

Budgeting for Change

None of this is an argument against change. It is meant only to show the background against which changes have to be viewed. Change is always a difficult objective. It automatically rejects what exists, together with the processes that keep that totality intact. In the present age, change is the major factor and must always be taken into account by financial managers. If they do not understand the changes that have taken place in their bailiwick, it is highly likely that they will fail to reconfigure their budgets to reflect those changes. This underlines the need for librarians to be aware of shifts in the financial universe every bit as much as of changes in the world of libraries, but, for the most part, library schools offer very little training in financial matters.

The budget, in reality, is a planning document. Rarely, if ever, do the plans of mice, men, or libraries go exactly according to the initial concepts. The "real" budget is the actual expenditures accounted for at the end of the fiscal period. The succeeding budget is often constrained by previous encumbrances and thus must take into account historical decisions. In this sense any budget should be considered as a guideline rather than as an exact template of what should be done. In the always-changing field of information, change rather than constancy is to be expected. How to deal with change should be the guiding idea. One outstanding example of considering the impact of change was the futuristic *Redesigning Library Services,* by Michael Buckland.[12] While we do not go so far in restructuring the library, we do acknowledge that the electronic revolution has completely redefined information, its means of access, and the appropriate role of the library. The needs of the mixed-information age are certainly different from those of an age when print was the principal source, but the actual needs of readers have not changed significantly.

One of the problems that must be resolved is differentiating between the means and the ends. This dilemma is the frequent subtext (to borrow a literary term) of much that is written about libraries. The movement to consider information as a commodity and library users as customers has become almost a given. While the authors do see the need to move from input to output measures, and the need to ensure that library policies serve their users, we also are aware that it is only too easy to slough off problems onto the difficulties of meeting once-in-a-lifetime needs, or the costs of providing special services. While the role of the user will be examined in more detail later, it would be useful for the reader to look up the very provocative article by John M. Budd in which he looks extremely carefully at the ways in which libraries have characterized both their users (the customer) and information (the commodity). He acknowledges the need for personalized service, but raises appropriate questions about the true relationships between institution, information, and the user, suggesting that it is only too easy for the institution to misdefine its customer base and thus its information or collection needs.[13]

The aim of this book is to examine these sometimes contradictory ideas and to point out ways in which libraries can best position themselves within the rapidly changing information world. The library budget has changed significantly over the last few years, often because the budget preparers have not understood the changes that have happened in the information world, but also because there has been little open discussion about the roles of the various participants in that world. Without such discussion these participants are likely to go forward without sufficient information as to what kinds of alliances or programs should be pursued. Wider discussion of the funding of information access can only benefit all participants.

Notes

1. Sheila S. Intner, "Ownership or Access? A Study of Collection Development Decision Making in Libraries," *Advances in Library Administration and Organization* 12 (1991): 1–38.

2. Barbra Buckner Higginbotham and Sally Bowdoin, *Access versus Assets: A Comprehensive Guide to Resource Sharing for Academic Libraries,* Frontiers of Access to Library Materials, no. 1 (Chicago: American Library Association, 1993).

3. Eugene L. Wiemers, "Financial Issues for Collection Managers in the 1990s," in *Collection Management and Development: Issues in an Electronic Era,* ed. Peggy Johnson and Bonnie MacEwan (Chicago: American Library Association, 1994), 111–20.

4. Elaine Goleski, "Learning to Say 'Yes,' A Customer Service Program for Library Staff," *Library Administration & Management* 9, no. 4 (fall 1995): 211–15.

5. David S. Sullivan, "Budgeting for Readers: Rethinking the Materials Budget," *The Acquisitions Librarian* 3, no. 2 (1991): 15–27.

6. Paul Metz, "Thirteen Steps to Avoiding Bad Luck in a Serials Cancellation Project," *Journal of Academic Librarianship* 18, no. 2 (1992): 76–82.

7. *Intellectual Property and the National Information Infrastructure: The Report of the Working Group on Intellectual Property Rights,* Bruce A. Lehman, Chair (Washington, D.C.: U.S. Department of Commerce, 1995).

8. During an interview, Paul Kobulnicky (Director of Libraries at the University of Connecticut) confirmed the predictions of Connie McCarthy that there would be a dramatic shift in the proportion of library budgets assigned to serials, saying, "I agree. Serials-based information is dying." See: Murray S. Martin and Paul Kobulnicky, "The Role of the Library in Institutional Development," *Bottom Line* 9, no. 1 (1996): 42.

9. Laura Kahkonen, "What Is Your Library Worth?" *Bottom Line* 5, no. 1 (1991): 9.

10. Herbert S. White, "Cost-Effectiveness and Cost-Benefit Determinations in Special Libraries," *Special Libraries* 70, no. 4 (April 1978): 163–69.

11. John A. Dunn Jr. and Murray S. Martin, "The Whole Cost of Libraries," *Library Trends* 42, no. 3 (winter 1993): 564–78.

12. Michael Buckland, *Redesigning Library Services: A Manifesto* (Chicago: American Library Association, 1992).

13. John M. Budd, "A Critique of Customer and Commodity," *College & Research Libraries* 58, no. 4 (July 1997): 310–21.

2

The Nature of Library Resources

Library resources include all print and print alternative publications. The question to be considered here is less their format than the conditions surrounding their acquisition and use. With this provision in mind, we can distinguish three classifications that cover the range of information items:

owned,

leased, and

accessed.

Each of these classes is subject to varying procedures and varying commercial and legal controls, whether one is speaking of acquisition or use. These differences can be used to help determine the role each kind of resource can play within the library. Each carries with it certain imperatives, and these have to be understood if the library is to allocate its resources properly.

Owned Materials

Libraries acquire by purchase and exchange, or obtain free, a wide range of materials: books, periodicals, maps, documents, records, and tapes, for example. Regardless of whether the library paid cash or value, or obtained them as part of an external relations program, the common element is that they are now owned by the library. This has important legal implications. Under the Doctrine of First Sale, there are now significant restrictions on the rights of the producers or publishers as to the use of their products. The library is able to lend them repeatedly, and, with due regard to copyright, the materials can be copied, at least in part. This may change, at least in respect to electronic publications, if Congress decides to follow the recommendations of the Working Group on Intellectual Property Rights.[1] The only other modification would apply in countries that have passed public lending rights legislation, which does not apply in the United States.

Copying Restrictions

There are some restrictions on the amount of copying that can be done by the library, but, so far, libraries acting in compliance with the copyright legislation cannot be held responsible for what their users may do. In Canada, this provision narrowly survived in the revision of copyright legislation. To be protected in the matter of self-generated copying, libraries will have to register with the equivalent of the Copyright Clearance Center.[2] Even in the United States, the classroom situation can be held to cover some kinds of copying that would not otherwise be permissible, but this is not truly the library's responsibility. Indeed, librarians are well advised to stay clear of this issue, which is entirely different from providing reserve reading and other kinds of reader service.

Performance Rights

There are also some problems with performance rights in the case of sound recordings on disc and tape. Reproductions of other performances may also be subject to certain restrictions. It is, for example, possible to make copies for archival purposes but *not* to preserve and keep the original unused, a real problem for music librarians, since many of these artifacts quickly go "out of print." This may be problematic for librarians interested in the preservation of the originals, but to most people it will seem like splitting hairs.

To the creators there is a significant difference. Replacement of the original brings in income; replacement of a copy does not. There is a significant problem here. Publishers, viewing the electronic market as a kind of bonanza, have tended to neglect the author's rights, forgetting that the copyright actually belongs to the author, and that electronic versions may be seen as parallel to film and television versions.[3] A further extension of this debate is the copying of videos, or radio and television programs, for classroom use. The present situation appears to be that such copies may indeed be made to accommodate classroom schedules, but cannot be preserved for indefinite use. Certainly they cannot be passed on to the library for safekeeping. One of the authors has had to refuse such a donation from a provost, who, as an author, should have been greatly concerned about intellectual property rights. These considerations forecast some of the problems librarians are certain to face with the expansion of electronic publications.

Such considerations aside, it would thus seem that owned or purchased materials form part of the library's capital expenditure and can be used repeatedly without infringing copyright. In this context, controlling authorities would be well advised to look again at whether the purchase of library materials is to be regarded as a capital or an operating expenditure. Purchased materials are, from this perspective, the institutions's property and can be used or disposed of as the library sees fit and are therefore capital in nature. This fits in with the First Sale Doctrine.

Leased Materials

Many databases (whether on CD-ROM or magnetic tape) are made available to libraries on a contractual basis. This is not universal but tends to be the norm. The library pays for the use of the materials in accordance with a contract or use agreement. In a sense, such materials partake of the nature of serials, since updates, additions, or completely revised versions are supplied at intervals, providing that the library pays its annual fee. If it should stop doing so, some contracts provide for the return of the original. Most do not, however, because the older the database the less valuable it is. The lease agreement can become very complicated, including, as it often does, hardware, software, and instruction manuals. Many accounting operations regard them as a kind of capital purchase or lease, because they often include hardware, and are unwilling to let the library proceed independently, even though there is little likelihood of finding alternative sources. Libraries should, therefore, seek the same kinds of exemptions as are usually applied to books. With recent legal decisions that have removed copyright coverage from such publications as Westlaw provided, there is some possibility of finding alternative publishers and better terms. Some contracts may even limit use to specified groups of users. This is especially common with business-oriented products, such as those produced by Standard and Poor's where use may be limited to students. This is an attempt to preempt free use by those who would otherwise have to pay.

Be aware that there are also many problems related to the use of "digital packages." There may be restrictions that derive from simply opening the shrink-wrapped package. Only too often, the controls involved are not made explicit to the general user. Some libraries make a practice of always contacting the seller to remove any onerous provisions. This can become very time consuming and costly and, for the most part, is unnecessary. Nevertheless all librarians need to be aware that these conditions exist and might be enforced in the case of blatant misuse.[4] Library patrons are unlikely to be aware of such problems and may infringe copyright unwittingly, which can lead to closer library oversight of their use. This then becomes a public relations problem that libraries must take into consideration.

More and more, these kinds of "purchases" are becoming subject to contract law, a very different situation from simple purchase. Added complexities derive from leases by consortia, which can achieve lower net costs, but which may also limit the degree of access available to an individual library, or may add to the processes needed to access the information. The important characteristic is that the library no longer has total control over the use of the asset. As always, librarians must decide what to do, based on the best interests of users. These issues were presented with great insistence by two speakers (Ann Okerson and Trisha Davis) at the 1997 ALCTS Preconference on "The Business of Acquisitions: Rethinking and Transforming Acquisitions."[5] As they said, librarians have to look carefully at what they are being offered by the various service vendors and see what effects there will be on their users. Prices and policies interact, but not always smoothly.

Mixed Goods

In some instances, there may be a kind of mixed good, where libraries contribute to a database (or a similar collective item, such as a union catalog or union list) and are, therefore, part owners. Prices and rules of use may not be under the control of the individual library, but it may have some influence over what is done. To some extent, this is the setting for bibliographic utilities and similar cooperative ventures. Who actually owns the data in OCLC Inc., for example, has never been resolved completely. The same is true for many other kinds of publications that aggregate information that is otherwise in the public domain, such as telephone directories, which may not be protected by copyright. In some cases providers of such compilations have taken steps to copyright headers on microforms and the like, to prevent indiscriminate copying. In answer to the concerns of its members, the Association of American Publishers is considering the adoption of Uniform File Identifiers (UFI) to serve as title page and copyright information on electronic files. These and similar methods of encryption add to the problems of libraries, which are acting as surrogates for their users, so that it may be necessary to distinguish the library and the individual user. By the way, such additions are illegal in France, which illustrates the added difficulties of operating on an international scale. The whole process of encryption is still subject to examination by international law.

These considerations become even more complex when there is a public/private mix of sponsors, where extensive privatization may well limit free public access. (Government data is an example.) This has already happened in New Zealand, where some census data, for example, are available only from private (joint) publication, and where commercial concerns have reduced the quality of some heretofore solely government publications.

Temporary Purchases

Leased resources could also be classified as temporary purchases. For a given sum of money, the library receives certain goods and has the right to use them on-site for the period covered by the contract. In some settings, other entities, such as the computer center, might become involved if it is a matter of downloading the data onto a central computer or a local area network (LAN), but these details do not dispute library ownership or control. Leased materials can be and are, to a great extent, regarded as purchases in that they are part of the library's collection and their use can be controlled by the library. In that sense they join owned materials as part of the public or common good, though with some restrictions on their use and with a different kind of cost structure. Because they are seldom available for outright purchase, these kinds of packages will continue to play a role in library collection development and library budgets and should be seen as part of the information resource budget. The way in which they are "purchased" may be affected by institutional or governmental regulations, but they should be regarded as largely similar to actual purchases in that they are for the general, not the individual, good. This concept has significant implications in terms of charges for their use. If they serve the common good, libraries should not expect to retrieve anything other than out-of-pocket costs, as they would for photocopying. This is a prime example of the problem of determining the public and proprietorial interests in any publication and its use.

Accessed Materials

In this chapter, "accessed" is being used in the relatively narrow sense of access to materials not directly owned by the library. The guidelines for the definition of such materials are becoming more difficult. Traditional access via interlibrary loan is relatively easy to handle, since it has a long history and significant case law.[6] Other uses, particularly of electronic materials, have not yet been similarly defined.

Under the Doctrine of First Sale, owned materials may be lent to others, including institutions, but may not be copied by such borrowers, nor should this process be used as a substitute for purchase. There are some exceptions in the matter of replacement pages for mutilated owned materials, but even these may have problems depending on the proportion of the original text being requested, always remembering that whole diagrams and illustrations are complete works in themselves. Because it has become increasingly common (and practical) to supply photocopies of articles rather than whole issues or volumes of periodicals, a series of guidelines has evolved from the copyright legislation and the accompanying Congressional record to protect authors' and publishers' rights—the Committee on New Technological Uses (CONTU) guidelines. In all such cases the copied materials are for the use of the borrower and pass out of the ownership and control of the library. This may not appear germane to budgeting for information resources but is part of the overall pattern of balancing access with ownership, and so must be considered when constructing a resource budget.

Budgetary constraints having reduced purchasing capacity for many libraries, it has become common for document delivery to be used as a substitute for purchase.[7] Whether or not the library pays the costs involved, the purchased material does not belong to the library. Moreover, the price paid may well involve both fees and royalty payments, as is the case with UnCover, Inc. and similar document delivery services. It is still, however, a matter of dealing with printed materials. Only the mode of purchase has changed. Instead of dealing directly with the publisher, the library now has to deal with a middleman, and, presumably, must absorb related costs.

Electronic Access

The handling of electronic access is an entirely different thing. The earliest kind of electronic transaction was dialing into a database maintained elsewhere, usually by a commerical entrepreneur. From small beginnings this has grown to a multibillion dollar business worldwide. A recent survey of 880 representative U.S. libraries by the Information Access Company indicated a substantial growth in site licensing, including nearly doubling by public libraries.[8] Here, each transaction is subject to a fee, whether individually or in terms of a bulk contract.

For the most part, until recently, the information recovered has been bibliographic, meaning that a further transaction has to take place to recover the actual publication. It is becoming more common for databases to include either abstracts or the full text of articles; e.g., InfoTrac, an early example where the articles were made available on microform. Although it would be possible for the library to retain copies of each search and any associated printouts, their one-of-a-kind nature makes this impractical and unrewarding. In many cases the nature of the contract rules out even the possibility. On the other hand, the library may itself conduct searches to produce consultable bibliographies on popular subjects, but such a procedure may run counter to the terms of the contract as being a kind of publishing venture, rather than simple use of the database. For the most part, then, libraries, when searching off-site databases, are simply acting as agents, and the results of the search pass to the requester. In budgetary terms this would seem to imply that the resulting costs should also be transferred to the user. This may not always be the case, when the libraries in question are trying to make up for cancellations. The issue then becomes what kinds of subsidies are appropriate and how they should be meshed in with other financial considerations.

On-site Databases

On-site databases are, however, governed by whatever conditions were set up by the lease. Apart from those considerations, libraries must also have regard to the operational costs, including the not inconsiderable cost of providing paper for printing. In this sense, the library has set up an internal site for the use of data provided by others, and has to be willing to meet the terms of its contract.

Whether the library recovers all or part of its costs relates less to the relationship with the information provider than to its agreements with its users. In the sense that these databases are equally available to all users, they share some of the characterstics of printed materials, but they also entail search-specific library expenditures much larger than the lending and borrowing of individual books. Most libraries have arranged for such actual expeditures as the printing of search results to be chargeable to the specific user, since that user has already had the opportunity to read freely the information in the database and any subsequent charges would parallel charges for photocopy. The presumption is that the individual user has benefited from open access and should, therefore, pay for that benefit.

Legal Issues

Many legal issues are involved here, following the nonresolution of the *Texaco* case, where the question was whether members of a corporation could copy and distribute materials to other members at distant locations without paying royalties or similar fees. Because the case was settled out of court, the legal issues involved were never determined. Only good case law can provide libraries with adequate guidance. The issue is of great importance to libraries with several branches, and to consortia where members may well be separated by considerable distances and direct user access to any one library may be limited.

- Can a library, for instance, send photocopy to a user at another branch or campus without having to think of the CONTU guidelines or other copyright considerations?
- Are distant users part of the same community or must they be considered nonmembers?
- Does a public library, acting for a local business in finding information, fall under the commercial class of user, thus being subject to stricter copyright controls?

While it may, at this point, be moot, the issue is certain to become more pressing as the amount of information available only in electronic format becomes greater. This does not imply that such accessed resources are not valuable, only that they are different. Indeed, libraries' participation in such arrangements is still a wise investment, since the library is buying the right to access data. A study of the impact of electronic journals conducted by the Massachusetts Institute of Technology Libraries suggested that there could be substantial changes in collecting practices.[9] This, in turn, suggests that libraries may well reconsider their collection goals.

Electronic Information Access

When we look at other kinds of electronic access, the picture becomes even murkier. With the development of the Internet it became possible to produce electronic substitutes for many printed communications. The most widespread use of the Internet is for e-mail, which continues the progression from direct, oral communication, through handwritten and typed letters, to the telephone conversation. Unless printed out, e-mail has only electronic existence and can, of course, be deleted by the author. This element of instability may become a major problem in the future because letters have been a principal source of information for scholars in many fields, not only in biography and history, and are of major concern to special collections worldwide.[10] The copyright implications are still not clear, although it appears that the same principles apply as to written or typed letters—the writer has the copyright. There are further scholarly concerns regarding the integrity of the text. As has been only too obvious, hackers can break into almost any file and distort it severely. This is an area where libraries, authors, and publishers have a very clear common ground and should be prepared to establish better controls.

Preservation Issues

Preservation, however, is still up in the air, and libraries should be concerned with its implications. Other kinds of publications, such as listservs, periodicals, databanks, reports, and so on may be covered by different rules. The owners may vary, there may be charges for access only or for downloading as well, and the rapid improvements in encryption devices may make pirating risky, if not impossible. Here there are entirely other kinds of issues, such as the ability to restrict access or to prevent copying altogether, and the question of who owns downloaded or printed out information. There are substantial differences between a purchased and a downloaded document. The former has clearly passed to the ownership of the buyer; the latter may not have done so. Some copyright experts advise that no one should pass on electronic information, unless they delete their own copies or take some parallel action to ensure that there are not multiple copies which would lie outside the general provisions of the copyright law.[11] None of these settings solves the problem of preservation, which still seems to lie with the originator of the information. As librarians have learned in the past, however, the author or publisher does not always take care to preserve the product, and the process is often left to the library community.

As the National Information Infrastructure becomes a reality we are certain to see more commercial publishing join what are now mostly public domain, or private (personal) publications. What rules will govern the use of these materials is still in question, but it is becoming clear that commercial online publishing will carry charges and fees, perhaps even a charge for browsing.[12] This changes the rules for libraries in collecting information and passing it on to users.

The Role of the Library

How far non-owned materials can be regarded as library resources is uncertain, since it is possible for anyone willing to pay the cost to link up and access the materials for themselves. The complexity of Internet use may militate against this, since access will require, for most people, the services of a mediator and that mediator is likely to be the library, or, more correctly, the librarians in the library. In this case the library *is* providing and paying for the access *and* providing an added value by way of organization and instruction. This kind of information resource is thus a kind of mixed good, neither material nor personal (service) but a combination of both. How this scenario will play out will be interesting to watch. Already, many of the larger commercial enterprises (e.g., Westlaw) are maneuvering to replace library intermediaries, particularly in special libraries, and this kind of development can be expected to increase.

It seems likely that electronic publications will be subject to the same kinds of differential charges that have long existed with regard to periodical subscriptions, with the possible difference that browsing may also be subject to some kind of charge. How libraries can manage this kind of change will determine their future place in the information hierarchy. Downloading and printing out, quite apart from their inherent costs in supplies, maintenance, etc. (not always explicitly encoded in accounting procedures), may also be subject to user fees or transaction charges. Librarians may be able to negotiate some kind of bulk service charge, but the fact remains that each transaction will be subject to some kind of cost.

As electronic publishing expands it can be expected to play an increasingly important role in "access" services, and thus will come to consume a larger proportion of the library's resource budget. It has even been suggested that the "access" share of the budget may become equal to that of serials, not because the budget has expanded but rather because access rather than ownership has determined the mode of expenditure.[13] This depends to some extent on the definition of access, but it also depends on the new ways of accessing information that are likely to emerge. There have been sufficient changes over the last few decades to ensure that there will be similar, and possibly even more extensive, changes in the decades to come. Libraries need to be concerned first with the rights of their users, and only secondarily with the rights of information producers.

Summary

All three kinds of resource—owned, leased, and electronically accessed—will be necessary if libraries are to meet their goal of "customer" satisfaction. Although many libraries and librarians seem to be saying that electronic information will meet all future needs, this stand is not always mirrored in the marketplace, where consumers appear still to want access to printed materials.[14] The trend toward electronic information clearly implies major shifts in budget allocations—not simply transfers between kinds of materials, but also changes in staff and operational expenditures, because of the different conditions controlling the use of each kind of resource, even while it remains necessary to maintain a basic printed collection. A resource budget is concerned with the entire library, not simply with library materials. It has become essential for librarians to think in terms of whole transactions and to look at alternatives, rather than to separate out specific kinds of expenditures. Again, this is a reminder that future library budgets must be user-oriented.

Notes

1. *Intellectual Property and the National Information Infrastructure: The Report of the Working Group on Intellectual Property Rights,* Bruce A. Lehman, Chair (Washington, D.C.: U.S. Department of Commerce, 1995).

2. *Feliciter,* the newsletter of the Canadian Library Association, provides updates on the progress of copyright legislation.

3. Margaret Bald, "The Case of the Disappearing Author," *Serials Review* 19, no. 3 (1993): 7–14.

4. This issue was addressed by Marcia Tuttle in a very amusing presentation at the 1996 Charleston Conference. She pointed out that one such purchase was still

on the university attorney's desk three years later, so complex were the issues involved.

5. The presentations involved were "Electronic License Policy: The Eternal Frontier," by Ann Okerson, and "Electronic Licence Prices: The New Frontier," by Trisha Davis.

6. Wayne Pederson and David Gregory, "Interlibrary Loan and Document Supply: Finding the Right Fit," *Journal of Academic Librarianship* 20, no. 5/6 (November 1994): 262–72.

7. V. G. Elliott, "Acquisitions and Access in Academic Libraries: The Case for Access Today, *New Zealand Libraries* 47, no. 10 (June 1994): 200–203; Murray S. Martin, "Cost Containment and Serial Cancellation," *Serials Review* 18, no. 3 (1992): 64–65; Susan B. Ardis and Karen S. Croneis, "Document Delivery, Cost Containment, and Serial Ownership," *College & Research Library News* 48 (November 1987): 624–27; Tina E. Chrzatowski and Karen A. Schmidt, "Surveying the Damage: Academic Library Serial Cancellations 1987–88 through 1989–90," *College & Research Libraries* 54, no. 2 (March 1993): 92–102.

8. "In the News," *Bottom Line* 9, no. 1 (1996): 48.

9. Marlene Manoff and others, "The MIT Libraries Electronic Journal Project: Reports on Patron Access and Technical Processing," *Serials Review* 19, no. 3 (1993): 15–40.

10. Stephen Jay Gould, in his review essay "The Power of Narrative," in *An Urchin in the Storm; Essays about Books and Ideas* (New York: Norton, 1987) regrets the passing of written communication, remarking that "the present can be a verbal wasteland." p. 76.

11. This point was made repeatedly at a 1996 seminar sponsored by ACRL/NEC where Arlene Bielefield and Lawrence Cheeseman, both experts in the area, warned librarians against assuming that there were no problems in making copies for others.

12. *Intellectual Property and the National Information Infrastructure.* There are few explicit references, but the tone of the whole document supports the idea that the user should pay.

13. Murray S. Martin and Paul Kobulnicky, "The Role of the Library in Institutional Development," *Bottom Line* 9, no. 1 (1996): 42.

14. Ingrid Eisenstadter, "A Tangled Info Web: Don't Be Deceived: Even a High Tech Library Still Needs Shelves of Books and Journals," *Newsweek*, February 16, 1997, 16.

3

Access and Its Implications

"Access" is an imprecise term, most commonly used to to refer to the use of materials not owned by the library. This begs the question of whether the use of owned materials could equally be termed access, since the individual user is, in a way, a part owner. Here we will consider "access" in its broadest interpretation as meaning finding, looking at, or using any printed or electronic information. As will be discussed in more detail later, access implies a very different approach to library organization than the older strategy of purchase. It also requires that librarians pay more attention to the mechanisms of creating knowledge. The difference between information and knowledge forms an important subset of library and information science.

The Relationship between Information and Knowledge

To a large degree, libraries have confused the terms "information" and "knowledge."[1] Strictly interpreted, information is simply data. These data can be factual or interpretative. Factual data, in the narrowest sense, are specific scientific facts, such as formulas, or recorded facts such as births, deaths, and marriages. Beyond this strictly delimited arena, data become subject to interpretation, a process that calls into action the process of knowing.[2] Knowledge is the product of the interaction of researcher and data. For the most part, this process is represented by publication and reading. Only in this format can data, or information, whether printed or online, have a true existence by becoming readily available to others; hence the importance of libraries as the repositories of shared knowledge. They provide a kind of marketplace for information, simply by their existence, but the added value of library activities has often been overlooked in the current rage to downsize any and all activities.

Knowledge in the World Marketplace

There are, however, some important caveats. Recently, researchers into economic growth have come to realize that knowledge—the understanding of information—is the basic issue in promoting corporate profits, to the degree that a new kind of officer has emerged—the Chief Knowledge Officer. This kind of change has not yet been understood by the library community even though it has been a staple of library services over the decades.[3] Great attention has been paid to the knowledge gathered by executives and other management officers over time, something that has not yet become common in libraries, where the hard-earned knowledge of information and sources that is the strength of professional librarians is often discounted in favor of using less expensive clerical and semiprofessional help. Staff downsizing or deprofessionalization may, therefore, interfere with the library's prime goal of spreading knowledge. For example, a library may lose the reference librarian's knowledge of the collection (which cannot be duplicated by the catalog) or the interlibrary loan librarian's accumulated experience with bibliographic and intellectual property problems. These are assets that cannot readily be replaced, and should be valued as part of the library's capital investment. They also illustrate the inevitable intermeshing of personal skills with published information. In the electronic world that is developing rapidly, these skills are even more likely to be needed, yet they are continually downgraded.

Information Recovery

Recovering data or information is a process basic to the nature of libraries. Any collection, printed or electronic, has no existence at all apart from the efforts of scholars and librarians to extract knowledge from its component parts. Unless that collection is adequately organized and properly described, individual researchers can have only fragmentary access to the totality of knowledge. As Penzias notes,

> Networked information access can realign fragmented tasks into more meaningful work. But even the most sophisticated technology is useless without human judgement and vision to direct an enterprise towards its goals.[4]

The importance of human intervention cannot be overstressed. This makes the creation of access or resource budgets much more complex, since they have to deal with all portions of the budget, not simply those allocated to materials, but also to personnel-related and support expenditures. These interact in ways that most budget setters cannot fully comprehend. The eventual need for a transaction-based budget is addressed in later chapters, but here it is important to emphasize that people and materials are involved in all library transactions.

What Is the Library Meaning of Information?

In this setting, what is the meaning of information? How is it possible to transform it into knowledge? To be accessible, information has to be organized. To retrieve it requires a joint endeavor between the researcher and the guardian, in this case the librarian. Although it may seem to be straining the point, readers may well ponder the lessons to be learned from a close reading of Umberto Eco's *Foucault's Pendulum* and *The Name of the Rose* and of Michel Foucault's *The Archaeology of Knowledge and the Discourse on Knowledge.*[5]

These, and many other works of literary and philosophical criticism, remind us that the relationship between information and knowledge is not a simple thing, amenable to the control of systems and organizations. Bridging the gap between ignorance and knowledge requires the application of the highest cognitive skills and the dedicated services of librarians. To simplify the quest by equating it with the mere recovery of specific artifacts undervalues the whole library enterprise. If librarians are, in fact, to provide the needed information they have to look beyond simple rules for the purchase and transfer of information. They will need to look at ways in which to assign costs, to allocate expenditures, and to evaluate alternatives in ways they have never done before.

The simplest kind of access is the setting in which the prospective user walks into the library and takes a book off the shelf. Simple, yes, but behind it lies an enormous amount of intellectual activity.

- First, the item itself has to be available—acquisition.
- Second, it has to be identified—cataloging and processing.
- Third, it has to be where it is supposed to be—shelf maintenance.
- Fourth, to be useful, it has to be described and given reality through a wide range of reference sources—catalogs, bibliographies, reference tools.

All these activities are basic to such a seemingly simple act as the retrieval of a book (or similar publication) from a shelf. That the same information may reside in an electronic equivalent does not reduce the need for the same processes; indeed it may even make them that much more important because electronic information does not always result in a readily identifiable artifact and may require even further categorization to make it accessible. To some extent, this resembles the need for cataloging and classification which many librarians have sought to downplay. Only full access to the appropriate descriptors can determine whether the specific artifact is truly what is wanted.

When a "book" is not available locally, a secondary tier of processes must be called into action. One has to determine, first, its actual existence (not always easy), then to discover where it is or is supposed to be, and, finally, to "import" it into the would-be user's world. When the "book" in question has only electronic existence, a fourth level of intervention is needed—its translation from electronic space to the space occupied by the user. Sometimes, especially in the case of such databanks as the U.S. Census or chemical composition information, it may also be necessary to translate encoded data into a usable format.

Here the data-to-information process comes closely to resemble the act of literary creation, and this is no less true if it is only necessary to transfer the electronic format to print. Clearly this need underlies many of the legal challenges to free access to electronic information. It will undoubtedly take time for legislation based on printed information to accommodate to electronic information, but librarians must not lose sight of the importance of the right of unrestricted user access. How this can be applied in a nonprint world is not currently easy to determine, but librarians need to act to preserve user rights.

The Economics of Information Transfer

These may seem to be unnecessary complications of an essentially simple process, but, if we do not understand what we are doing, it is unlikely that we can design our library systems to achieve the appropriate results. The advent of electronic information has been seen as a kind of relief from an increasingly difficult balance between the need to purchase wanted items and the (in)ability to pay for them. If it is "out there" in electronic format, or if various systems can be used to import the needed material, the pressure on the local budget can be reduced. This is a simplistic response to an increasingly complex problem. Although we have, for a long time, treated information as free, it is now clear that it is not, or, at the least, that its retrieval costs money. Since libraries are constrained by the amount of money they have available to respond to users' needs, it is becoming increasingly necessary to make the most financially responsible choices about how to meet those needs.[6] These choices are now made more difficult by the different kinds of rules that accompany the different kinds of media, most notably printed and electronic resources. Libraries need to be aware of these differences and how they affect their ability to deliver information to their users. Library budgets and the results need to be constructed in such a way as to forward rather than thwart information transfer. They need to make it simple to repond to a user's need, whether for print, electronic information, or the interpretation of that information.

Printed Materials

Printed materials form the simplest and most direct part of the information universe. Though they may be costly or difficult to obtain, they have a simple existence. Once in the hands of the user they can be read and studied, and can be used over and over again without the investment of too great an amount of library time and expenditure, following the legal Doctrine of First Sale. There are problems with their preservation, some papers having a very short physical existence. There are problems with knowing whether they exist or can be found. They can sometimes exist in multiple copies or editions, and it may be necessary to differentiate between these, but, by and large, once printed, a book has a definite existence and can be traced and used. The library may or may not own a specific book, but has the ability to see whether it is available elsewhere with a fairly sure knowledge that it will be what the user wants.

There is also the fact that in many parts of the world printed information will remain supreme for many years to come because the inhabitants of those countries cannot afford electronic publication and access and can make much more efficient use of printed materials. It is, for example, possible that the supply of electricity can be cut off without warning, and that the library or individual has no guaranteed access to any specific service. This has profound implications for any international projects, where the sharing of information is essential, and raises the issue of information deprivation not only for individuals but for entire countries and cultures. These issues have been understated in most considerations of the information needs of advanced countries.

Electronic Publications

Electronic publications, however, have no similar physical existence (apologies to our physicist friends) and exist only in a coded or digital format, accessible through the use of various programs and software applications. While this may seem to be the equivalent of print, it has to be remembered that no process yet exists to ensure that no changes have been made in the contents or their arrangement. Publishers and others are working to ensure some kind of integrity, but this also revolves around commercial and legal rights.[7] Moreover, anyone who has generated an electronic publication can equally as easily destroy it, so that it then has no existence at all (and never had?). What then becomes of research based upon such documentation? This is by no means a hypothetical situation. Anyone using an electronic file will discover that some of the contents can disappear without warning. Even worse, the contents may not have been updated for years, leaving a very false impression of the current situation. On a simpler level, electronic information that needs to be used over an extended period of time has to be translated into some kind of usable format, whether by downloading or by printing. Each of these processes imposes a further need, either on the user or on the supplier (in this case, the library), to pay for the cost of translation.

- Once translated, is it the same artifact, or has it taken on a separate existence?
- What kinds of costs and payments such as royalties are involved?
- Who is responsible for these?

These relationships are keys to the electronic information age and need to be resolved. The respective roles of the library, the supplier, and the user need to be reexamined closely. They interact so closely that this may be difficult to determine, but the effort must be made.

Information Recovery Costs

Even this simple a venture into the nature of information reveals that there are many questions for libraries to answer when it comes to budgeting for the recovery of information. The easiest answer is to buy the particular item needed, but it is true that, if it is never needed again, the library (or more properly its supporting community) has paid the cost of an individual's request for information. Most library materials do not fall into this category, since they are used several times by many different users, at a minimal cost per use. The cost per use, however, can vary dramatically. One use per year of a journal costing $3,000 *is* $3,000; ten uses of a book costing $30 average $3 per use, in both cases discounting the minimal cost of the actual circulation process. This is not as fanciful as it seems, since the usage rate of some of the most expensive journals is extremely low, while inexpensive popular books may be used until they self-destruct. This point was made very forcefully by Charles Hamaker at the ALCTS Preconference in 1997. He cited many references to the low document recovery rate for cancelled serials, and further articles suggest that his findings are correct. Out of the 2,500 cancelled periodicals at Louisiana State University, only 130 titles had five or more requests for articles, while 423 had two to four requests, and 740 titles had only one request for an article. This suggests that as many as half of the cancelled serials never had been used in the library. He further offered the information that for the 1,300 articles requested from the 130 most popular titles, the subscription cost was $89,995, and the document delivery cost was only $20,968.[8] The difference is staggering, though it must be remembered that other costs are involved in the recovery of wanted articles.

The same kinds of arguments can be used to examine the use of electronic materials, though here there are even more additional costs to consider. Books and the like have very few added costs, mostly in the nature of space costs, which may now be about $7 a year per volume. Electronic resources carry a wider range of ancillary costs, such as equipment to use them, software to retrieve them, electricity to run them, staff to assist in their use, and the cost either of downloading or printing. There have been almost no studies of such costs and it would be difficult indeed to derive them from regular library budgets because most of the telecommunications costs involved are buried in a wide range of budget lines, not all of them assigned to the library or controlled by the library.

The many queries about the practice of charging for printouts and the increasing difficulty of paying for free access make it clear that libraries are realizing that even this end product has its budget problems. Free downloading is somewhat like buying and giving away books, but charging can also be seen as depriving some people of the right of access.[9] Far from being the solution to budget problems for libraries, electronic access has simply added a new layer of difficulties. Chief among these may well be the guarantee of the permanence of electronic publications and their possible transfer to electronic archives. The scholarly community is presently engaged in a discussion about the merits of electronic publication, about the need for standards for such publications, and about how to transfer the present standards for review, editing, and evaluation from the print world to the electronic world. These are not issues outside the library agenda, but speak directly to how effective the library can be in transferring information, since it is likely to be the final repository for all scholarly publishing, whether in print or electronic format, no other participants in the process having been designed as archival repositories. If they are to perform this function or service, they should at least be entitled to know whether the materials in their care are, in fact, the final versions.

Budget Formulas

There have been some attempts to deal with this problem. Older formulas for the distribution of the library materials budget within academic libraries dealt only with printed formats—books and serials. Some efforts were made to develop "volume equivalents," for example, for microforms or phonograph records, but these were simply nibbling at the edges of a far greater problem. Typical approaches looked at how to develop ratios or proportions for spending money on library materials. This was often encouraged by the manner in which institutional budgets were constructed. The oldest formulaic ratio is called the 60:40 ratio: 60 percent for serials, 40 percent for books. Even this begged the issue of where to place standing orders for annuals or multivolume sets and required the elaborate projection of volume equivalents for such kinds of publications as microforms, videos, and other media. As prices for serials continued to rise faster than for books, this approach became untenable, and libraries tended to move toward 70:30, even in some cases 75:25.

It should be realized that the fault lay not in the use of ratios and formulas but in the radical changes that were taking place in the publishing world. Because there were differentials between book and serial price increases, a generalized increase to provide for inflation automatically depressed the book portion of the budget. This had disproportionate effects on different parts of the materials budget. The impact of price increases was larger on the scientific and technological portions of the budget, and correspondingly less on the humanities and sociological portions, even though these areas of publication have seen some sizeable price increases.

Books vs Serials

Clearly, this created an impossible situation, since there was no diminution in the numbers of either kind of publication, and budgets were no longer rising to meet inflation, in some cases were actually falling. The Association of Research Libraries statistics show quite dramatically that the member libraries' purchases of books were falling rapidly, causing a reduction in the overall pool of information available within research libraries.[10] At the same time, ever-increasing expenditures on serials were not maintaining the same numbers of subscriptions. It was at this juncture that the idea of purchase equivalents became popular. Instead of buying, it might be possible to "access" information. Since the budget available was not growing, access could come only at the expense of ownership, meaning that acquisition funds would be diverted to pay for "purchase on demand," interlibrary loan, or document delivery.[11] This in turn would mean a further weakening of the owned collection, causing a kind of downward spiral. There are serious questions regarding the effects of serial cancellation programs, no matter how difficult the financial circumstances that caused them.

Several studies suggest that many major cancelled serials were never used, but that others in the "marginal" category were sorely needed but were subjected to some kind of "across-the-board" reduction process.[12] The process has now gained a momentum of its own as a kind of panacea for insufficient funding. It has been suggested that the new distribution is likely to be 30:30:40, with access and serials each taking 30 percent of the budget.[13] The important factor here is the recognition that books will remain a necessary element in the provision of information. A different perspective is provided by Linda Brown, who suggests that "there may not be a single 'right' way to set priorities for serials access and ownership. What's important is that priorities *are set* and articulated."[14]

Universal Access to Information

While strategies like this may be possible for an individual library, they do not deal with such issues as maintaining access to the whole range of human creativity, or who will be responsible for ensuring that there is universal coverage. Indeed it may be that universal coverage and accessibility will become even less possible as libraries are forced to economize. Only the emergence of well-planned cooperatives will enable users to maintain access to the information they need, and that is one more budget item for libraries. Many earlier strategies such as the Farmington Plan[15] were abandoned because of the costs involved, but it is clear that research collections are tending to resemble one another more closely, with many marginal interests being reassigned to access rather than to ownership. This will be examined more closely in the chapter dealing with cooperative action, but it is necessary to understand that this kind of access can carry with it substantial retrieval costs. If a needed item is not owned, the library has to decide whether to pay for its retrieval or to charge the individual wanting it. Because of these factors, access has become a much more far-reaching element in library planning. While libraries, especially public libraries, will clearly continue to purchase materials, they will also have to devote more funds to access. The proportions will continue to be debatable, and librarians will have to look closely at how each element fits into both their missions and their budgets. Only this kind of examination will enable libraries to participate fully in the future information age.

Summary

Access implies the existence of a body of information organized to permit individual users to find what they want. The library best fulfills this definition, but current budgetary and managerial directions seem to be undercutting this relationship. True, the problems of enabling all users to gain access to and use of the materials they need (the two are different) may push the library beyond the relatively simple boundaries of an organization that acquires and then lends materials wanted by its users. In particular, electronic publishing has created a new library world, where the exact relationships of creator, publisher, user, and library are no longer so clear. Budgets based on ownership may no longer best serve the library. Instead, it may be necessary to develop budgetary concepts that include charges for information use and reimbursements for the originator of the information. In a way this implies that libraries will have to behave in a businesslike manner; not that they have not done so in the past, but that now they will have to look very closely at the financial implications of their policies.

- How possible will it be to protect universal access to information when it may be necessary to pay for each individual use?
- What does this do to the equality of each user, if the poor can readily be disenfranchised?

Libraries and their controlling authorities will have to look very carefully at these potentially socially divisive factors as they plan their responses to the rapidly evolving universe of information. The issues range far beyond whether libraries should charge for certain services and engage the library profession in a discussion of what its true role is in the age of electronic information.

Notes

1. Richard Abel, "Information Does Not a Library Make: Three Outrageous Propositions," in *Issues in Collection Management: Librarians, Booksellers, Publishers,* ed. Murray S. Martin (Greenwich, Conn.: JAI Press, 1995), 1–18.

2. Arno Penzias, *Ideas and Information: Managing in a High-Tech World* (New York: Norton, 1989). For another example of how the scientific community looks at information in formulating its canons, librarians may find some interest in Stephen Jay Gould's *An Urchin in the Storm: Essays about Books and Ideas* (New York: Norton, 1987), which consists of reviews of seminal books in the biological sciences.

3. Tom Davenport, "Think Tank: Knowledge Roles: The CKO and Beyond," *CIO* (April 1, 1996): 24–26; Stan Davis and Jim Botkin, "The Coming of Knowledge-Based Business," *Harvard Business Review* (September/October 1994): 165–70.

4. Penzias, p. 213.

5. Umberto Eco, *Foucault's Pendulum* (New York: Harcourt Brace Jovanovich, 1989) and *The Name of the Rose* (New York: Harcourt Brace Jovanovich, 1983), and Michel Foucault, *The Archaeology of Knowledge and the Discourse on Knowledge* (New York: Pantheon, 1972).

6. Kenneth J. Bierman, "How Will Libraries Pay for Electronic Information?" *Journal of Library Administration* 15, no. 3/4 (1991): 67–84.

7. The Association of American Publishers (AAP) is working on a kind of identifier, which can be used as the equivalent of the copyright symbol, designed both to

protect the publisher's rights against illegal use and to maintain the integrity of the document. The process of encryption has yet to gain universal approval, but may well be necessary to protect individual privacy in the electronic world.

8. The presentation by Chuck Hamaker was on document delivery. Further documentation is available from Lynne C. Branche, "Document Delivery: Where Collection Development and ILL Meet: An RASD Collection Development and Evaluation Section Program," *Library Acquisitions: Practice and Theory* 18 (1994): 96–97; Tina E. Chrzastowski and Mary A. Anthes, "Seeking the 99% Chemistry Library: Extending the Serials Collection through the Use of Decentralized Document Delivery," *Library Acquisitions: Practice and Theory* 19 (1995): 141–52; Jane P. Kleiner and Charles A. Hamaker, "Libraries 2000: Transforming Libraries Using Document Delivery, Needs Assessment, and Networked Resources," *College & Research Libraries* 58, no. 4 (July 1997): 355–74; Eleanor Mitchell and Sheila A. Walters, *Document Delivery Services: Issues and Answers* (Medford, N.J.: Learned Information Inc., 1995).

9. The cost of access to the Internet is seldom made the matter of extensive consideration; yet, by reading between the lines of reports of grants and state subsidies for the initial connection, it is possible to deduct that the ongoing cost can be substantial, sometimes beyond the capacity of the library budget. In a recent budget decision about the support of a public library known to the authors it came down to a choice between money for materials or for electronic access to other library catalogs for interlibrary loan. This is a false tradeoff, since the library's budget for acquisitions was totally inadequate for even its basic needs.

10. Annette Melville, *Resource Strategies in the 90s: Trends in ARL University Libraries* Occasional Paper no. 16 (Washington, D.C.: Association of Research Libraries, Office of Management Services, 1994).

11. The "Scholars' Express" initiated by George Washington University and since adopted by other research libraries is an example of this kind of response, where savings from subscription cancellations were set aside to provide funds for retrieving needed articles. The major planning benefit was that this amount became a permanent part of the budget.

12. The earlier citations in note 8 apply, as do the more wide-ranging surveys by Susan B. Ardis and Karen B. Croneis, "Document Delivery, Cost Containment, and Serial Ownership," *College & Research Library News* 48 (November 1987): 624–27; Tina E. Chrzatowski and Karen A. Schmidt, "Collections at Risk: Revisiting Serial Cancellations in Academic Libraries," *College & Research Libraries* 57, no. 4 (July 1996): 351–64; and "Surveying the Damage: Academic Library Serial Cancellations 1987–88 through 1989–90," *College & Research Libraries* 54, no. 2 (March 1993): 92–102; Eleanor B. Gossen and Suzanne Irving, "Ownership versus Access and Low-Use Periodical Titles," *Library Resources & Techncial Services* 39, no. 1 (January 1995): 43–52.

13. Murray S. Martin and Paul Kobulnicky, "The Role of the Library in Institutional Development," *Bottom Line* 9, no. 1 (1996): 42. The ratio itself was projected by Connie McCarthy of Duke University in an informal communication. Other studies of ratios and projections of future budgets include Jerry D. Campbell's "Academic Library Budgets: Changing the 'Sixty-Forty' Split," *Library Administration and Management* 3 (1989): 77–79, and "Getting Comfortable with Change: A New Budget Model for Libraries in Transition," *Library Trends* 42, no. 3 (Winter 1994): 448–59.

14. Linda A. Brown, "Balancing Information Needs with Serials Values and Costs," *Against the Grain* 9, no. 2 (April 1997): 22–24, 26, 28.

15. The Farmington Plan grew out of a recognition during World War II that the country's holdings of foreign publications were deficient; it was an effort to assign collecting responsibilities by country to the various members of the Association of Research Libraries. This plan was later accompanied by the various Library of Congress foreign acquisition projects (P. L. 480), which were also designed to provide materials for other libraries, and by the Latin American Cooperative Acquisitions Plan. Most of these are now defunct. They were intended to guarantee American access to foreign materials, but carried with them an overhead cost that could not be maintained.

4

Resource Sharing

Resource sharing has become a kind of library shibboleth, with the implication that the entire universe of information can be at hand, painlessly. Nevertheless, the history of coordinated acquisition (e.g., the Farmington Plan), suggests that the issue is far more complex than simply wanting it to exist.[1] In 1973, the first national conference on resource sharing in libraries took place at the University of Pittsburgh, sponsored by Allen Kent, whose later study of library use at the University of Pittsburgh Libraries earned him a great deal of attention[2] even while it engendered the 80/20 rule,[3] which has since become widely adopted. In the decades since that time, there has been little to indicate that libraries are prepared to consider rational proposals for the shared development of collections, even though, as suggested by Buckland, it is not entirely satisfactory to answer that a copy exists and is being carefully preserved in some foreign national library.[4] This may seem somewhat condescending, but illustrates the problems that can lie at the end of the resource-sharing road.

The Pittsburgh conference prepared to face the kinds of problems that have now become endemic to all libraries, but the response to any suggestions of coordination or sharing was, at best, lukewarm. There was, for example, no response whatever to an offer, made by one of the authors of this book, to establish a shared fund for marginal acquisitions. In retrospect, this was not the most effective approach, especially now that electronic publication and resource sharing have become so popular, but at that time there were few alternatives, and the response suggests that most librarians were less concerned with achieving the best level of service than with protecting their budgets. This attitude has scarcely changed since then, even though it may now be disguised under the rhetoric of electronics.

In fact, a similar program sponsored by the Boston Library Consortium foundered several years later because no individual library wanted to be responsible for holding common resources and making them available. The promises and pitfalls associated with state library networks were explored at an ASCLA meeting at the American Library Association Conference in

31

San Francisco in 1997. Some of the problems were identified as similar to building an airplane while it is taxiing down the runway, illustrating the difficulties involved in a continual learning process.[5] Yet, the totality of information can be accessed only by the use of many libraries and other services. It is not possible for any one library to provide all that its users want. The corollary, that some libraries will have to purchase materials that will not have wide local use, is a deterrent to resource sharing. Unless all libraries are willing to specialize to some degree, vast quantities of publications will fall out of the public arena. This facet of resource sharing has not been adequately addressed, even by the research libraries of the world. It may be as simple a task as the New York Public Library assumed, when it sent out a staff member, every so often, to purchase the latest sex periodicals so readily available on 42nd Street, but it can be as complex as trying to ensure that the publications of third-world countries are not relegated to some kind of collecting limbo.

Collection Duplication

The fact is that most research libraries tend to replicate significant portions of one another's collections, since they are using the same kinds of strategies geared to similar curricula.[6] This is understandable but certainly does little toward preserving the entire universe of knowledge. Similarly, public library cooperatives, in seeking to reduce costs, often rely on dealer plans or publisher-generated pools. These strategies help reduce library acquisition costs but also reduce the range of publications acquired. There is, for example, great concern as to whether outsourcing will still provide first-rate collections suitable for the library's users. The almost spiteful response to the decision to outsource buying for all of Hawaii's public libraries, while it had some positive impacts, such as the need to be responsive to local interests, overlooked the fact that direct selection and purchase of all needed titles is now almost economically impossible.

More recent outsourcing agreements seem to indicate a kind of rapprochement that will deliver more locally acceptable service. Overlap studies suggest that there is more variability than these statements may imply, but earlier reports from OCLC also show that there are many fewer holding libraries, even for the most popular titles, than one might imagine.[7] Problems with methodology (cataloging is not always accurate) may make these reports suspect, but it is hard not to conclude that, for at least some kinds of materials, there are not the extensive holdings of individual titles that might be expected. The library world should pay more attention to this kind of data and seek to determine how effective resource sharing can be in a world where libraries are increasingly pressed for cash to buy materials.

Collection Specialization

One mitigating factor is that, within any group, each individual library will have some kind of specialty that separates it from its partners. An example is the Fenway Library Consortium, which includes members as diverse as the Museum of Fine Arts and the Wentworth Institute of Technology. Because of this diversity, the total collection available to consortium members is as great as that of a research library of some size. Again, a survey of the holdings of the Boston Library Consortium libraries revealed that each had something unique to contribute to the whole, often out of proportion to its apparent size.[8] These events came about by chance rather than by design, and the results could easily be changed by individual library collecting decisions. Unless the cooperating libraries agree on some method of deciding on what will be acquired or discarded, there can be no guarantee that the entire range of materials will be preserved for general access.

Discards

Discarding "previously owned" materials, to borrow a phrase from the used car business, presents a particularly difficult problem, especially for public libraries, whose goals do not usually include long-term preservation of all information, and there have been very few examples of any coordinated efforts to ensure the retention of last copies, for example of popular fiction. Academic libraries have tried to set up such programs, but have had little success because of the complex actions involved. The result may, however, presage a future information access problem when researchers seek to find materials that have been discarded without adequate thought. For example, a study by Harley C. Brooks on the availability of Westerns in libraries revealed that there was no way in which any researcher, scholar, or general reader could be assured that the whole corpus had been preserved.[9]

Serial Cancellations

In hard budget times, academic libraries have generally cancelled "marginal" subscriptions, often without any consideration of whether they may be unique.[10] Marginality is in the eye of the beholder. What is marginal from the perspective of a budget-cutter may be essential from the perspective of a researcher. Interestingly, subsequent library records often indicate that many journals of record are seldom used locally. Research by Lynne Branche Brown indicated that of the 2,000 journals cancelled by George Washington University, articles from only 300 were requested.[11] Too often, more credence is given to the big departments or users, and their needs are given priority, even though the expenditures involved may be very large indeed.

Many of the most expensive sci-tech journals are simply journals of record and could as easily be used in the form of databanks, which may become a reality if some of the projects suggested by Elsevier gain general acceptance. The first step toward this new setting was taken by OhioLINK, which cut a deal with Elsevier Electronic Subscriptions for a three-year contract to supply electronic versions of all 1,150 Elsevier Science journals. The total cost was $23 million, the equivalent of the current subscription costs to the participating libraries. OhioLINK will store the electronic versions, which will then be accessible to all members. The important factor here is that this access expands almost exponentially access to information by the smaller member libraries, which may only have had 10 to 13 subscriptions. A secondary factor is that all participating libraries will no longer have to pay the costs associated with maintaining paper files.[12] These costs are not inconsiderable—but will the savings be offset by added costs for downloading and printing out requested articles? The latter may require additional agreements about who pays for what services.

At the other extreme, many of the inexpensive journals in the humanities are essential for the extension of their disciplines. They are inexpensive because most of the work that goes into producing them is free, not because they are "marginal." Moreover they are much less amenable to databank conversion because their content requires extensive reading and comparative study. Issues of this kind are seldom taken into account when it is time for budget cuts.

Libraries also need to be continually aware of the range of needs of their constituents. Electronic information is *not always* the preferred answer, and the kind of user need—intensive or extensive—can affect library plans. This kind of differentiation lay behind the appointment of disciplinary or subject specialists in academic libraries, but budget problems have caused a kind of backward movement toward generalists. As Linda Brown points out, "there may not be a single 'right' way to set priorities for serials access and ownership. What's important is that priorities *are set* and articulated."[13]

Resource Availability

Resource sharing, in whatever form, depends on the availability of the resources to be shared. In other words, if one library does not own them, another must. Whether these resources are in print or electronic format is of little immediate consequence—though the costs associated with retrieval may have later budget consequences. One prominent librarian in the field of Australian studies claimed that it was possible to rely on international interlibrary loan to make up for deficiencies.[14] For one library or for one program, that might be possible, but, if the principle is extended to all libraries supporting similar programs, it soon becomes a *reductio ad absurdum* when we all come to rely on the unique copy held in one library somewhere in the world.

Interlibrary planning has seldom led anywhere of importance; witness the many hours spent on assigning collecting responsibilities among Research Libraries Group libraries, reduced simply to talk by budget stringencies. Moreover, any such scheme will still depend on the work of individual librarians in selecting materials. A more realistic model, based on *Choice,* as described by Rodney Erickson, suggests that more can be accomplished by smaller groups of libraries having either close geographic connections or more similar missions.[15] The goal of universal access will depend less on grand schemes and more on careful budget and acquisition planning. At least, libraries now have the benefit of direct access to the various union catalogs and union lists of the bibliographic utilities—with the caveat that withdrawals are seldom adequately reported—and do not have to work as much in the dark as in earlier days.

Information Transfer

Sharing implies a way of achieving that goal. Many of the suggestions outlined here will be treated in more detail later. The oldest established method is by using interlibrary loan (ILL). In itself, ILL is a marvelous device, but has been more and more downgraded in the face of such wonders as document delivery, electronic transfer, and commercial purchase on demand services.[16] ILL is still essential for materials in lesser demand or held only by a few libraries, for whole publications such as books, or for those items for which bibliographic data are insufficient, requiring rather the study of the actual materials. Moreover, there are still no reliable alternatives for materials with extensive illustrations (particularly in color), or many graphs and diagrams.

Document delivery is simply a fancy name for some of the things ILL used to do, and increasingly it involves commercial services. Certainly it can accomplish seeming miracles, for example the success rate in using a service such as UnCover Inc., but it also carries a price which may be greater in the long run than simpler alternatives. Also, such services work best when they are dealing with high-volume use, rather than with once in a lifetime needs, or with materials that are obscure and difficult to retrieve. In true entrepreneurial manner these services are likely to skim the cream off the market, leaving libraries, and their users, with the problem of looking after the skim milk. Downloading from electronic databanks carries with it the same kinds of problems, and adds new ones. Not only will libraries have to face the difficulty of negotiating copyright thickets, they will have to face the cost of either downloading or printing out the information required.

Of course, many of these issues are being addressed in innumerable meetings and settings with the active participation of all parties. So far, there seem still to be two sides to the debate, the producer (though mostly the publisher, rather than the author[17]) and the consumer. The direct consumer, however, is scarcely present, at best being represented by the libraries. Although much government rhetoric is directed toward the idea of each schoolchild being able to access the information superhighway—for example speeches both by President Clinton and Speaker Gingrich—little of substance has appeared behind this rhetoric. What access means and what is being accessed have conveniently been forgotten. The more mundane negotiations about the nature of the National Information Infrastructure reveal a wide gap between supplier and user.[18] Will there be access charges, and who will pay them? Such practical questions are being swept aside in the general fascination with the enabling technologies. Unless libraries can restructure their budgets to handle such issues, it will become increasingly difficult to include within the library's range the wide variety of information-seeking and -finding technologies that have recently emerged.

Support Structures

Librarians, over a long period of time, have attempted to find ways by which to address the gap between where the users are and where the information they want is. The early development of union catalogs and union lists is adequate testimony to this quest. Other methods have included the rise of various *consortia* and *networks*. Consortia are groups of libraries that get together to promote common needs. Networks first began as agencies to promote easier sharing of such services as cataloging, acquisitions, etc. such as those provided by OCLC, and have since become important sources for cooperative endeavors like shared training, the development of regional resource sharing, and the production of regional databases. Without such network support most libraries would be hard pressed to provide the services necessary to keep their staffs up-to-date. These networks are now looking toward an increased role in the provision of shared information. This movement will undoubtedly progress by fits and starts, since there are far too many players for simple, universal solutions. The OhioLINK/Elsevier contract refered to earlier in this chapter suggests a possible direction for library collectives, but is far more expensive than smaller groups of libraries could afford.

Technology and Networks

Automated library system vendors have added to this support structure, both by providing training and by encouraging member libraries to work together. In addition, local system vendors and bibliographic networks have encouraged member libraries to participate in the development of shared systems, of course, with some realistic expectation of increased profitability. This mix of entrepreneurial "go get 'em" expertise and libraries' sense of their need to look beyond their own boundaries has resulted in many kinds of technological advances, such as are represented by OCLC's FirstSearch and PromptCat, or RLIN's development of Ariel.

System vendors now make a selling point of their provision of access to various databases, or the fact that their systems provide resource-sharing subsystems. The general result is that vendor/utility/library interactions are now much more complex, making it that much more difficult to determine what each has contributed to the whole. Despite this difficulty, libraries now exist within a much more complicated support structure, which makes it hard to withdraw unilaterally from a business relationship without upsetting their service goals.

Among the most exciting of the recent commercial ventures is UnCover Inc., a document retrieval service developed first under the aegis of Colorado Assocation of Research Libraries (CARL), a library-originated automation system, that is now completely self-sufficient in commercial terms. Its aim is to offer libraries access to articles and other information, as, for example, the *Choice* database of reviews and the use of a wide range of evaluative materials, including personal book reviews.

The catch, if that is what it can be called, is that these articles are retrieved from library collections, now international in scope, thanks to the participation of Blackwell's International, but subject to access fees and to the payment of royalties to the publishers or other copyright holders. A library using this service may well be able to supply information on demand, but must decide whether to absorb these costs or pass them on to the user. Some libraries have opted to reduce subscriptions and thereby create a fund from which to meet these costs (e.g., MIT), but others believe that they are not in a position to take this kind of action. The question is still who should pay? While the consideration of fee-for-service activities is outside the direct scope of this book, it has to be realized that such issues underlie the adoption of any budget strategy, whether tacitly or explicitly. Many public libraries are now considering fees for electronic reference services, or for telephone reference, and these practices can be expected to spread. While not thought of as being related to the collection development budget, such services have an impact on collecting policies, particularly for electronic materials.

Cost Effectiveness

The new technologies that have made it much easier to transfer information, whether by fax, computer, or the U.S. mail, have opened up a whole new range of issues relating to cost and payment, along with the original provision of the service. This raises several relationship issues such as:

- Who should pay for what?
- Does the library have a responsibility to supply materials it does not own without charge, or are such services beyond its charter?
- What kinds of costs should be passed on—direct, out-of-pocket costs only, or the total cost of the transaction?
- Should there be an attempt to limit the numbers of such transactions, perhaps for specific classes of user (e.g., students are exempt from charges but faculty are not, or costs can be charged to businesses but not to individuals)?

The resolution of such questions has become more difficult in the wake of the nonconclusion of the *Texaco* case referred to in more detail in chapter 2. Settlement by Texaco left unresolved just what nonprofit institutions might be able to do.

- Is it justifiable for a public library to charge local businesses, because it is a commercial transaction, but not to charge an individual who could, in fact, be acting on behalf of a commercial enterprise?
- What are the copyright implications of either decision? What happens to fair use?

The San Francisco Public Library has recently joined the ranks of public libraries offering fee-based information services to business, industry, and the local municipality, but some of its own staff have had reservations about whether this may affect free access to information by poor individuals. The service concentrates on specific business information needs, seeking to supplement the firm's own information activities. The Sunnyvale Public Library, also in California, has set up a joint project with other local and national firms to provide specific information such as patent searches. These services are clearly in demand, but are extending the older definition of the role of the public library.

The justification often offered for charging a fee is that the library is providing added value, but then could not all library services be construed as a form of added value? On the face of it, it seems relatively easy to justify charging users who are receiving faster or more comprehensive service, but if libraries had to recover all costs it might be far more difficult to justify the library's very existence, other than on social grounds. The issues surrounding the provision of a public good are not going away; in fact, they may become even more prominent. In a recent decision the Wellington City Council (New Zealand) decided that 90 percent of the library's benefits were public and 10 percent were private.[19] How this decision was arrived at was not made clear, but it resembles the kind of approach described by Yvette Tilson, where libraries in the London area were expected to raise a certain proportion of their budgets from revenue.[20] This kind of approach can be expected to increase and suggests that there will need to be closer assessments of the costs and benefits of sharing.

Cost Studies

To help even to begin to resolve these issues, librarians must be prepared to undertake more rigorous studies of their costs. Interlibrary loan activity has been studied to death.[21] On the other hand, reference and acquisitions have not been subjected to the same rigorous examination, and nobody has looked at the costs of selection or computer system development with the same close scrutiny. Since all these activities are involved in the provision of information access, all must be taken into account when studying alternatives, and require a much closer cost scrutiny.

While, at first glance, public, school, academic, and special libraries may seem to inhabit separate worlds, their activities are governed by the same kinds of economic rules. They receive a budget and, in return, provide certain services. The congruence between these two is seldom investigated, other than in the most general terms, such as collection growth or circulation. In fact, they exist in a complex world where some activities are easily quantified and others are not. Costs do not necessarily equal values, and it is the value placed on library services that is most important when attempting to determine whether it is cost-effective. The problems in dealing with cost and value are little addressed in budgetary procedures, but they are basic to determining what kinds of investment the institution in question is prepared to make. Most institutions do not seek to resolve the issue of what contribution their sectors make to any project.

- If a college can encourage a winner of a Nobel Prize to join the faculty, and part of the attraction is the library, how much is the library worth?
- If a public library can help a local business to improve its performance, or help the unemployed to find new jobs, how should that performance be reflected in its budget?
- If a special library assists a researcher toward a new breakthrough, or aids in making a new sale, should its contribution be recognized financially?

All too often cost and value are confused, as are efficiency and effectiveness.[22] The library's problem is that its product is diffuse rather than concentrated, and that, consequently, it is difficult to assign a cost to any specific action. This may be changing, as libraries use more sophisticated budget models, but these too have their costs. Value, moreover, is assigned by the user and not by the library. These problems make for great difficulty in defining the proper role of the library, and equally so for setting up its budget.

Library-User Dialog

The problem of assigning both value and cost implies a much deeper dialog between library and user. Both have a role in determining the part the library should play. Some questions one might ask are:

- Does the library have a responsibility to provide all possible information?
- Does it, therefore, have to bear the cost of providing that information?
- Does the user have a responsibility in determining what information is necessary?
- If so, should the user pay part or all of the cost?

The assignment of these shares will determine what proportion of the cost the library should bear. The resolution of these problems has been made more difficult by the production of user-friendly computer-based aids. InfoTrac, for example, provides both bibliographic access and files of the materials analyzed. The role of the librarian is thereby apparently diminished, but there are still maintenance costs—and the undetermined issue of whether the user is being well served by a very selective database. An ongoing issue is the role and value of the librarian. What does he or she contribute to the resolution of information needs, either directly or indirectly?

Personal Roles

The same issues surface time and again.

- What is the actual role of the librarian in this new universe?

- What is the role of the user?
- Who can determine when both need to work together and when the best results are obtained by leaving the user on his or her own?

Because reference and similar services are very labor intensive, libraries are tending toward leaving the user alone. At best, libraries fulfill an apparently marginal role by providing user-friendly artifacts; at worst, they seem to fade into the background, since few realize that the library is needed to keep those artifacts functional. Further, many areas of intellectual activity are not, at least currently, well served by automation alone. These are the areas where there is a need for older materials, or where the examination of an actual publication is essential, for example in the editing of literary texts. There are other areas in the social sciences and the humanities where there are, as yet, few comprehensive automated tools, and where it may not be possible to transfer publication to an electronic medium.[23] Libraries need to take these situations into account when deciding whether to charge for services or to take responsibility for providing them. This statement is not meant to suggest that the process of determining the role of resource sharing in a resource or access budget is easy, only to show the kinds of factors that must be considered.

Models for Resource Sharing

There are many models available. Most are voluntary, depending on individual library action to achieve their goals. Some states, for example, Pennsylvania, have set up a layered set of libraries, from local to district to regional, giving the latter subsidies to support collection development in specified areas. In Alabama, on the other hand, libraries agreed to make their collections mutually available without any specific direction as to collecting. The now dismantled Farmington plan assigned collecting priorities to members, but finally the complexity became too great. At one stage, for example, the Cornell University library had thousands of uncataloged Icelandic materials simply because that country had been assigned to it for collecting, regardless of the cataloging capacity available. Fortunately, Cornell has recently come to an agreement with Iceland to develop a digital preservation project for the most important materials. The Research Libraries Group sought to determine member interests and priorities, but the program foundered because it was too difficult to implement. Interestingly, similar proposals have been made in New Zealand, where the National Library has redefined its collection priorities, leaving it up to other libraries to fill in the gaps. It is generally clear that such massive schemes have had little success in the long run, because they become too complicated and may well run foul of individual institutional goals, even as a shared serial cancellation program proposed by the Boston Library Consortium failed because individual member libraries could not agree on how to implement it.

Although this may seem to be dismissing shared resource development, it is intended simply to underline the complications. Libraries need to continue cooperating, because no one library can possibly buy all it needs for its users. Most of the programs indicated above were initiated in simpler nonelectronic times, but they show how difficult it is to blend the needs of multiple institutions. Most academic institutions are now participating in many joint programs, and it is not always possible for libraries to harmonize the resulting needs. One library has even reported participation in more than 100 shared programs, which could be incredibly difficult for circulation and interlibrary loan to sort out. The great expansion of distance learning can be expected to exacerbate this problem, as it becomes very difficult to decide whether the user in question is an internal or an external patron and to decide what kinds of charges or procedures to use. Libraries will continue to experience this kind of difficulty and need to develop ways of coping with its effects.

Summary

The need to access resources held elsewhere will continue to be a major factor in determining what a library can or will do within its budget. Unless access is relatively easy, users will tend to opt for what is available locally, perhaps denying themselves essential information. This is becoming increasingly the case with electronic databases, which students and even faculty will use in preference to the arduous task of looking at actual books and articles by themselves. The library, as go-between, is caught up in this process and needs to develop models based on the value of its transactions, rather than on the costs of the various inputs. While the virtual library (or digital library) is almost certain to develop at some time in the future, for the moment ordinary libraries are still necessary as intermediaries in the retrieval process. While they can share resources and they can share services, someone, somewhere, has to pay for them.

Notes
1. Michael Carpenter, "How Can We Improve Resource Sharing? A Scholar's View," *Advances in Library Resource Sharing* 1 (1990): 59–73; "If We Say Resource Sharing Is a Good Thing, Let's Mean It," *Journal of Academic Librarianship* 17, no. 4 (September 1991): 230–31; Richard Hacken, "The RLG Conoco Study and Its Aftermath: Is Resource Sharing in Limbo?" *Journal of Academic Librarianship* 18, no. 1 (1992): 17–23; Anna L. Price and Kjestine R. Carey, "Serials Use Study Raises Questions about Cooperative Ventures," *Serials Review* 19, no. 3 (1993): 79–84.

2. Allen Kent and others, *Use Study of Library Materials: The University of Pittsburgh Study* (New York: Dekker, 1979).

3. The 80/20 rule is the widespread belief that 80 percent of the need can be met by 20 percent of the collection. The problem, of course, is that nobody can possibly know in advance which book or other item is part of the golden 20 percent. Libraries have responded to decreasing budgets by shifting from buying materials "just in case they may be needed" to buying them "just in time" after

a need is established, a major change in their philosophies of purchase, though there are no studies yet that show how effective this has been. The formula was derived from business, but has been applied widely in the measurement of library activities, and even *distorted* to imply that attaining an 80 percent fulfillment rate, say in interlibrary loan, is sufficient.

4. Michael Buckland, *Redesigning Library Services: A Manifesto* (Chicago: American Library Association, 1992), 56.

5. *Cognotes* (June 29, 1997): 8.

6. This can be deduced from reliance on gathering plans and similar arrangements, which almost guarantee that libraries in the same kind of setting will have a major overlap between their collections. It is the differences that are important but, so far, these have not been studied.

7. See, for example, "The Most Popular Books of 1993" (*OCLC Newsletter* ([March/April 1994]: 8–11) in which the highest recorded number of holdings was 1,670 from more than 24,000 participating libraries.

8. Ann C. Shaffner, Marianne Burke, and Jutta Reed-Scott, "Automated Collection Analysis: The Boston Library Consortium Experience," *Advances in Library Resource Sharing* 3 (1992): 35–49.

9. Harley C. Brooks Jr., "The Availability of Western Series Fiction in American Libraries," Collection Management 17, no. 4 (1993): 49–56.

10. Murray S. Martin, "Cost Containment and Serial Cancellations," *Serials Review* 18, no. 3 (1992): 64–65; and Tina E. Chrzatowski and Karen A. Schmidt, "Surveying the Damage: Academic Library Serial Cancellations 1987–88 through 1989–90," *College & Research Libraries* 54, no. 2 (March 1993): 92–102.

11. Lynne C. Branche, "Document Delivery: Where Collection Development and ILL Meet: An RASD Collection Development and Evaluation Section Program," *Library Acquisitions: Practice and Theory* 18 (1994): 96–97.

12. "OhioLINK Cuts $23 Million Deal with Elsevier for Journals," *Library Journal* 122, no. 11 (June 15, 1997): 12.

13. Linda A. Brown, "Balancing Information Needs with Serials Values and Costs," *Against the Grain* 9, no. 2 (April 1997): 22, 24, 26, 28.

14. A comment made by Ross Atkinson at a meeting of the Australian Studies Discussion Group, during the American Library Association Conference in San Francisco, June 1992.

15. Rodney Erickson, "*Choice* for Collection Development," *Library Acquisitions: Theory and Practice* 16, no. 1 (1992): 43–49.

16. Wayne Pederson and David Gregory, "Interlibrary Loan and Commercial Document Supply: Finding the Right Fit," *Journal of Academic Librarianship* 20, no. 5/6 (November 1994): 263–72.

17. Margaret Bald, "The Case of the Disappearing Author," *Serials Review* 19, no. 3 (1993): 7–14.

18. *Intellectual Property and the National Information Infrastructure: The Report of the Working Group on Intellectual Property Rights,* Bruce A. Lehman, Chair (Washington, D.C.: U.S. Department of Commerce, 1995).

19. *Library Life Te Rau Ora* 211 (April 1997): 13.

20. Yvette Tilson, "Income Generation and Pricing in Libraries," *Bottom Line: Managing Library Finances* 8, no. 2 (1995): 23–36.

21. The most recent report is that by Marilyn M. Roche, *ARL/RLG Interlibrary Loan Cost Study: A Joint Effort by the Association of Research Libraries and the Research Library Group* (Washington, D.C.: ARL, 1993), but there have been numerous cost studies dating back to the 1970s. Readers should be aware that these have generally concerned major research libraries and may not always be easily applicable to other situations.

22. Brian Nielsen, "Allocating Costs: Thinking about Values: The Fee-or-Free Debate," *Journal of Academic Librarianship* 15 (1989): 211–17.

23. Brett Fairbairn, "The Present and Future of Historical Journals," *Journal of Scholarly Publishing* 27, no. 2 (January 1996): 59–74.

5

Information Alternatives

At times, it would seem that librarians are prepared to desert print-based information in favor of electronic alternatives. This may seem to be a surface view, but only too often statements in the literature suggest that print is dead. As suggested by Charles Meadow, the book may certainly have a future, though it may well be changed, even enhanced by technology.[1] The question must be how realistic is this shift, in the short term and the long term? Print is a firmly based medium with a long history. It offers several things not readily available in an electronic format; e.g., the ability to refer back easily to earlier statements and the ability to compare one source with another without having to move from one program to another. Moreover, at least for some time to come, it is not economically feasible to transfer many kinds of printed resources to an electronic medium, particularly for publications with limited audiences or eclectic reference materials. Finally, it is highly unlikely that the vast numbers of existing original artifacts (novels, plays, and the like) will be transferred to electronic formats within the near future. The issue here is not the need to preserve such materials through the process of digitalization, but the question of whether regular publishing will move from print to electronic format.

Printed Publications

Print sources are likely to remain a major budgeting component for libraries for some time into the next century. Admittedly, most such sources are being generated via computers rather than typewriters or typesetting, but the problems involved in developing electronic versions go far beyond simply whether they can be made readily accessible via Internet.[2] Developers of such products must take into account whether their use will be sporadic or intensive, intermittent or continuous, whether it will require close attention to detail or the comparative checking of content and definitional entries. The latter is particularly problematic because of the wide range of protocols governing the input of bibliographic information.

In a larger context there is the problem of comparing, easily, the "facts" set out in one encyclopedic compilation as against another. Until all national protocols have been brought into conformity, it will continue to be difficult to be sure that the exact reference has been traced. This also involves the issue of whether the correct document has been retrieved. The matching of citation and publication has become a great deal more complex in the electronic information age. Problems of this sort were the subject of several poster presentations at the American Library Association conference in San Francisco in June 1997, and are not to be downplayed because this process is central to the conversion of information into knowledge. It is still difficult to ensure that the current text is the same as previous texts, because there is no monitoring service such as is provided by the editorial processes for printed materials.

Information Transfer

Deriving information from printed or electronic sources requires substantially different modes of operation. Books and other printed media can readily be copied and annotated. Electronic publications require a totally different kind of mediation. Downloading, which can be cost intensive, simply transfers the information from a source to an individual file. Sorting out what may be relevant and transferring it into a manageable datafile may also require printing, again an expensive investment. Even if the work in question is being carried out electronically, there is the need to ensure that the data in question are accurately transcribed and properly paid for—royalties, transcription costs, and the like. This process is time-consuming. Indeed, it may prove almost impossible for the publishers of electronic books, as distinct from periodicals, to maintain any kind of control over what is available or not available, the online equivalents of in print or not in print, and even more difficult to ensure that there are not multiple versions "out there." This concern is likely to be addressed by all the concerned parties, if simply from economic reasons, but the solutions will be difficult to find, if the past history of negotiations over such topics as electronic reserves are any guide.

What Is Likely to Be Available?

While some reference-type files may never be profitably transferred to print, largely because of the low numbers of potential users, others continue to hover uneasily between print and electronics. Publishers must consider carefully their purchaser base.[3] Can they jettison print users in favor of electronic users? The latter are most likely to be corporate (in this context libraries are corporate users), and the loss from personal purchases or subscriptions may well overweigh the benefits accruing from corporate purchases.[4] The same is likely to be true for any book purporting to synthesize the last decade's work in any subject. Moreover, any abstract or philosophical treatment of a subject is likely to continue to be more user accessible in a printed format because its reading is more likely to be based on leisurely contemplation than on the "need to know." All these arguments are compounded by the problem of addressing the need to read and contemplate creative writing. Novels, plays, poems, and essays are not readily transferable into the electronic canon, at least not until many of the problems associated with electronic consultation are removed—at best a subject for science fiction at this moment. One must wonder at the ease with which future intergalactic wanderers can call up any information they need and expect that it will be properly organized and indexed, though this is the scenario in many SF novels. The extreme difficulty of doing this now may be transformed in the future, but the prognosis that it will happen soon is, at best, optimistic.

The present laborious process of reading a lengthy electronic text and the difficulty of referring back easily to an earlier page are simple examples of the problem. Although many proponents of online information seem to imply that all information is equal, a closer reading of the user population suggests that there are wide variations in audiences and that these audiences have differing needs. This is the element to which libraries have always paid attention and the one that distinguishes them from bookstores and other commercial information outlets.

What Should Be Saved?

There are many kinds of information that have no lasting value other than in a historic context, for example, today's stock prices. Many current news stories, similarly, need to be recalled only when wanted. Much of this information is available in various databanks, appropriately so because there is no need for thousands of libraries to maintain shelves and shelves of printed versions. That does not decrease the need for libraries to hold the current printed versions. It indicates only that permanent retention is not necessary. In fact, when libraries can provide only outdated versions of such publications as directories, they are providing misinformation. The same is true of electronic publications, only too many of which are not updated regularly, largely because the process has turned out to be onerous and time-consuming.

The underlying budget issue is the most appropriate format the library should acquire. The answer will differ by subject and reader intention. Many thematic reference sources, for example, are highly unlikely to be transferred solely to an electronic version, if only because that would unduly restrict the numbers of purchases, whether institutional or personal. The library that fails to purchase an appropriate selection of these publications could be called reference poor.[5] Despite the increasing interest in CD-ROM, tape, or other electronic versions of fiction and similar publications, at least partly because of the different social settings involved in their use as against the private nature of reading, there is no reason to believe that most readers will want to move from print to alternative formats, and the same is likely to be true for many children's publications. Reading is a basic skill, needed for other intellectual endeavors, including the use of electronic resources. Without the ability to read and to continue practicing that skill, people could find themselves losing other skills. Television screens and other electronic products do not help a great deal in maintaining reading skills, because much of their message is transmitted pictorially or orally.[6]

Preservation Issues

The retention and preservation of printed materials raise several issues that are marginal to the main purpose of this book, though there are clearly budget issues involved. Weeding and discarding older materials have long been library practice, especially for public and special libraries, and justifiably so in light of the costly nature of library space, which should not be wasted on little- or never-used materials. There has, however, been lamentably little coordination of such discards. Reliance on major research libraries is not enough, particularly when it concerns popular or practical materials. For instance the National Library of New Zealand announced recently that it would no longer be responsible for maintaining a collection of international fiction, and this would have to become the shared responsibility of other libraries. One of the authors was particularly saddened by this development, since he spent many years helping to develop that collection. Preservation is an even more urgent matter, particularly for books and serials published on nonpermanent paper, indeed perhaps the whole world of paperback books.

Printed materials are likely to endure as a library staple for some time to come and must continue to receive an appropriate budget allocation. What this ideal proportion should be is not yet clear, but, in the academic library world at least, it is likely to remain at the traditional 40 percent and could be even higher in public libraries, particularly for children's materials, adult leisure reading, or large-print materials. These settings remind us that there are occasions where the specific qualities of printed information are essential for the use in question.

However, because of the large numbers of such publications, libraries will always have to be aware that they cannot purchase and make available everything a potential user might want. Here, alternative access protocols enter the picture, whether to electronic alternatives or simply to borrowed printed (or photocopied) materials. No matter what the method, if the transaction is to be successful, the needed material must exist somewhere, in whatever format.

Electronic Publications

Despite the bias apparent in the previous paragraphs toward print, it is clear that, in many areas, electronic publication offers a much better future. Where several layers of factual information are melded or supersede outdated or inaccurate information, electronic publications are ineffably superior to printed versions. Similarly, evanescent publications such as newsletters, circulars, or bulletins can best be provided electronically. Historical preservation is another issue, not germane to the present discussion. The same is true for such things as stock exchange reports, monetary conversion rates, or complex census data. Where meaningful information, as distinct from scads of accreted data, is desirable, electronic programs, with almost instant editorial capacity, are far to be favored over the complex and time-consuming processes of print consultation. This condition is most likely to apply to business and financial information, where volatility is the rule, though it must always be recognized that historical research may have different needs.

A further strength of electronic records is their capacity for compiling and compressing past information into a presently usable format. *Thomas's Register* and Standard and Poor's publications can, in their printed format, provide an unrivalled snapshot of the situation, but, as most of us know who have tried to get in touch with individuals or corporations, change rather than stasis is the rule—even as far as changed area codes, telephone numbers, and personnel. To keep on top of such volatile settings, only electronic media can cope. Be aware, however, that these are as subject to update failure as any printed source. This was made clear by the decision of the Somers Public Library to cancel its subscription to an electronic telephone number database in favor of a CD-ROM, because the latter was more accurate,[7] as well as being cheaper. Even so, the cost of maintaining several shelf feet of printed publications tends to outweigh the cost of providing additional personal services, such as calling directory service for an update.

The Nature of Databanks

Some kinds of databanks are never likely to reach printed format, for example in the humanities, where a Dante thesaurus is unlikely to have a wide enough purchasing base. This says nothing as to their scholarly value, only that the marketplace is too narrow for traditional publication without substantial subsidies, and those are tending to be drastically reduced over time.

Others are too complex to be successfully encompassed in print. Although Information Services Inc. (ISI) still produces a wide range of *Current Contents* in a number of subject areas, it is only possible to cross-fertilize a search electronically, while searching through years of monthly issues is a labor-intensive task. An instance where this characteristic was put to good use comes from the University of Delaware which substituted, with the cooperation of the faculty, a document delivery service as a substitute for purchased serials. Although the *Library Journal* headline may be somewhat optimistic about "solving budget woes," this kind of approach demonstrates neatly one way of balancing both ownership and access, and publisher sales and leasing.[8] A further example is *Chemical Abstracts,* which is far more accessible in its electronic format. Publications such as company annual reports and balance sheets represent an impossibly wide spectrum for any library to organize and catalog. Far better to subscribe to an electronic version. Unfortunately, the same does not apply to art exhibition catalogs or auction catalogs that contain many illustrations, both of which may be as important to people in their own areas as bank statements and profit-and-loss accounts are to those in business. While this situation may yet be resolved, it would appear that, for some time to come, there will be areas where printed information remains superior.

In other instances, librarians must take into account the level and amount of usage. If a periodical title is little used, electronic access may well be the better solution.[9] Indeed, many journals of record are little used, but each library must look at its user needs. Smaller libraries may find that access, even if royalties are paid, turns out to be the better bargain. Such decisions should always be made carefully, since they depend for their validity on an evaluation of the uses actually made.

Looking at Alternatives

Any library is faced with determining whether there *are* print and electronic alternatives, and which is the most appropriate for that library. A realistic survey of the alternatives available to libraries was presented by Ross Atkinson, who has always been a strong proponent of the book, when he suggested that access and ownership must continue as partners.[10] In some areas the decision will be clear. In others, it will not. To some extent, the choice will have to be based on cost, both institutional and individual. CD-ROMs and similar databases may require special software, and access to online databases can be quite costly.[11] If, as seems possible, even browsing electronic publications will become subject to a charge, librarians will have to think very hard about substituting electronic for print access. Maintaining both may well provoke a budget crunch, but neither one may meet all user needs, because of the differing nature of each medium. The following questions need answers:

- Who is to be served—those who can pay for a search, or all persons in need of information?
- What kinds of charges should be levied—total recovery of costs, or out-of-pocket costs only?
- Can libraries charge for access to public data? The U.S. Census data provide a very good example. If much detailed data are available only from electronic records, will users be able to pay the cost or will they be deprived of access to public records?
- Can the library absorb the cost of such access?
- Should the library absorb the cost for all or some users?

In other countries, for example New Zealand, much census data is now available only from privately printed sources.[12] This trend can only be expected to increase. In the United States, some institutions have reacted to this situation by forming consortia, and this trend can be expected to increase. The participating libraries have to keep in mind the costs of belonging to one or several such groups.

Other Media

Microforms, multimedia publications, digital preservation, and the like have become common forms of publication. In some settings, for example the maintenance of newpaper backfiles, they make sense, both because of the space saved and because the originals deteriorate rapidly. The result, however, is a double subscription cost, plus the cost of projection equipment and services. Something else that should be kept in mind is whether the total publication is to be preserved. For example, *The Hartford Courant* has a local news section for each area served. Can or should all such sections be included in the microform version, or will one central repository be sufficient? The adequacy of the microform version must be considered, e.g., for back-runs of periodicals. This is particularly important where there are many illustrations in color. Where the original printed version is in poor shape, with close-cropped margins and poor printing, a microform version may not be able to compensate for the deficiencies, and a photocopy may prove impossible. Moreover, some microform or electronic copies leave out advertisements and even multipage special inserts, and many periodicals adopt a rather strange version of pagination that omits advertisements, even though the latter, from a library point of view, are important sociological documents. Any institution wanting to maintain a file of airline periodicals (for example travel and advertising agencies) would find this a nightmare.

Multimedia Collections and Their Problems

New multimedia publications offer so much more access, via chained references and pictures, that they may well overtake traditional publications in selected areas where the need is to access a wide range of information in multiple formats, for example in schools. The drawback is that they are expensive to prepare and also depend for retrieval on adequate hardware and software, which are added costs to the library. Many encyclopedias and dictionaries have moved into this format, though sometimes with added charges for individual use. The added value is new forms of retrieval. The drawback is that, unless the library can afford to install and pay for multiple reading stations, only one person at a time can use the new publication, whereas several users could look at individual volumes of a multivolume print version at the same time. Moreover, many users will want the convenience of being able to flip back and forward within a printed volume, something not always readily available in electronic format. The intellectual danger with the electonic approach is easy acquiescence to the preselection of the information to be made available.

Collection Maintenance

The maintenance of large collections of slides, pictures, and similar illustrative material has long been a problem to libraries. Until a few years ago, few alternatives were available. Now, however, microform publishers have been able to produce excellent colored reproductions, and these may well offer libraries new ways of providing such materials. Reproduction locally may still be difficult, but at least users can look at pictures they would not otherwise have been able to see. In part, also, these publications may help reduce the problems associated with the theft and mutilation of printed books. Many art libraries have had to impose strict rules for the use of illustrated materials (e.g., Princeton University), and one of the banes of interlibrary loan has long been the wish by users to copy borrowed materials, totally contrary to the rules of copyright law. If the library can supply art materials on microform, some of these problems will be reduced. There are still hardware problems. Only too many microform sets are now unusable because the needed equipment is no longer available. The other aspect is that microform versions are not readily accessible from home and office locations.

Microform or digitized publications are also able to provide a much better means of access to complex issues, because they have had to undertake an initial subject analysis before publication and can include the access codes, references, and the like that went into developing the publication. Some of these, however, may be subject to restrictions on use, such as being separately copyrighted. This can apply even to such apparently innocuous additions as headers on microforms. Nevertheless, these publications are here to stay and libraries have to consider their place within the library's acquisition program.

Databases

Databases comprise a quite separate category of publication. Most are acquired via contract rather than purchase and may be subject to special conditions. These conditions may prescribe who can and cannot use them, whether there are fees for downloading or printing, and whether the library has ownership or simply leases the contents. There may also be fees for commercial use, the existence of which is not to be lightly disregarded. Is a public library, acting on behalf of a local company, engaging in commercial use? Academic libraries have sometimes found it advisable to transfer sensitive economic databases to the business school, where control of its use is simpler. Until all the issues surrounding the use of electronic resources have been resolved, libraries may well be advised to take a lower profile.

In the present information environment, however, libraries will have to be much more proactive in the procurement and use of databases if they are to serve their user groups. There is some evidence that this is happening.[13] Two kinds of relationships are developing. The first is through purchase or lease; the second is through access. Purchase or lease of databases is likely to be confined to larger libraries and consortia. Most local libraries will simply provide users with access, in which case they will also have to decide what charges, if any, to levy on users, i.e., out-of-pocket costs only, or the total cost of access, including staff assistance? Moreover, there are other kinds of databases, not always considered such, like access to a regional or consortial catalog, where the library has an interest but is unlikely to be able to charge for use, because it represents a local investment. Here the issue is extending local access and providing better service, rather than attempting to expand income. For a fuller investigation of some of the cost issues involved see *Setting Fees for Services in Libraries,* by Murray S. Martin and Betsy Parks (New York: Neal Schuman, 1997) and the numerous articles and news notes on librarians' attitudes toward fees.[14]

Media Relationships

Libraries have to determine the benefits of holding publications in various formats. When it was simply a matter of deciding whether or not to buy a particular printed publication, the decision was relatively simple.

- Was the book appropriate to the library's mission?
- Did the library have the necessary funds?

If the answers were affirmative, the library would purchase it. With the advent of new media the decisions became more complex. Some, for example videotapes, were simply substitutes for "books." Others, such as microforms, could be either substitutes or alternatives for printed materials. Electronic publications, however, represent an entirely different kind of issue. In a sense, they can never be purchased. Even subscriptions to electronic journals are not truly purchases, unless the subscription allows for downloading. Here the issue becomes what format will be most useful to the library user. A study of these relationships in New Zealand, where financial and distance concerns are both important, suggests the emergence of a new synthesis. Wooliscroft meshes collecting and service responsibilities.[15] Since most databases will only be leased or accessed, not bought, this further expands the ramifications of providing information.[16] It is no longer clear what rights inhere in a subscription if the subscription is electronic, and it is difficult to ascertain what kinds of responsibilities the subscribing library has assumed.

Budgetary Implications

The effects of these decisions on the library budget are wide-ranging.

- How much of the library budget should be directed toward accessed rather than owned publications?
- What are the effects of adding microform, CD-ROM, or similar alternatives, or of using them to substitute for print publications?

The most obvious effects are operational. All these media require additional telephone lines, equipment, software, or hardware to make them accessible to the user. Are these capital expenditures that require other kinds of procedures such as bidding out, or should they fall in the library materials category where the librarian is generally considered the expert? This leads to the consideration of where they should show up in the budget. So far, there is little agreement over that, but it seems likely that yet another category should be added to the library materials budget, since some may be similar to serials, or to one-time purchases of major works. Others, however, go into the same category as bibliographic utilities, being purchased services. This leads to severe difficulties in comparing library budgets when differing decisions have been made by the responsible accounting authorities. This is further evidence of the need for more study of the costs of the various alternatives available to libraries.

Budgeting for Alternatives

It is also true that some of these choices will overlap, at least in part, either with already owned printed materials, or with one another. Some budget-driven administrators may see this as a bad move, and will question what they see as duplicative expenditure. Surely, if you already have the book, you do not need another format, or, if you have electronic access, why do you need all those other publications? While these questions seem naive at present, in the future they will become more pertinent as electronic publications become more comprehensive and more available.

It is possible to argue that they represent different *levels* of access to information, and that some formats are more appropriate to some users than others, in much the same way as a children's book can provide an entirely satisfactory introduction to a topic for an interested adult who does not want to be overwhelmed by scholarly prose. Another argument is that many publications supplement rather than replace others. It may be perfectly appropriate to have massive collections of early government documents, travel narratives, or collections of letters on microform, but the beginning, or even the experienced user, will need to use guides or summary publications to initiate a search. An archive of photographs or pictures from historical sources would be out of price reach for most libraries other than in microformat, and therefore an unlikely purchase. But they exist, and their use requires access to studies of the artists and other creators involved, studies which generally exist only in print. This reinforces the interactive nature of the various media collected by libraries and used by scholars or the general reader.

These kinds of relationships will vary with the subject matter, but suggest the complexities of operating within a multimedia future. They also suggest some of the future problems facing consortia, since the sharing of some kinds of materials will differ greatly from simply being able to send them through the mail or a delivery service. Although online access may seem the obvious solution, it does nothing to address the problems relating to shared use of resources, since it presumes that all can access the records equally. Some of these relationships are indicated in Figure 5.1, which sets out some of the interactions and relationships in terms of the rather more traditional library organization. Personal and automated responses to user needs lie in between collection development and resource sharing, and act as a kind of directional mechanism. The whole forms a continuous circle or ellipse, which suggests that each action will have an effect on other actions. This reflects the problems

FIGURE 5.1   Reference and Information Functions

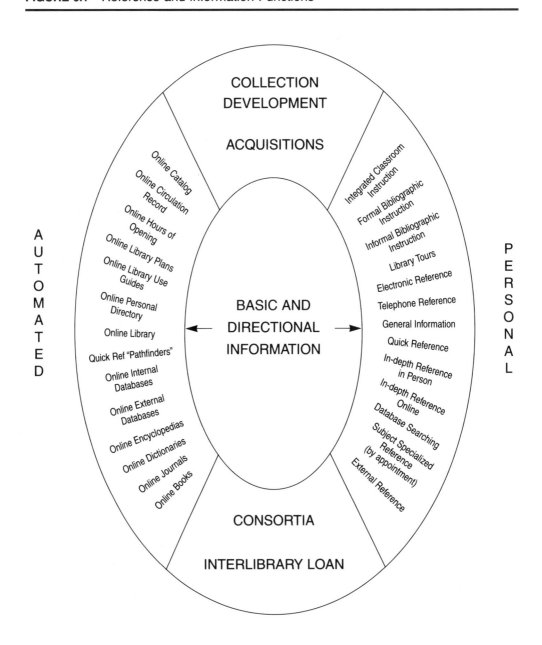

faced in developing an effective budget approach, made all the more difficult because libraries are not usually well structured for horizontal communication and consultation.

Another way of looking at this relationship is shown in Figure 5.2, which looks at the interrelationships between specific library functions and adds various overhead considerations. Here the important factor is the interrelationship between these transactions and the surrounding support services. The effects will almost certainly differ between transactions, but if the various factors are not taken into account, it will almost certainly be impossible to establish any hierarchical values. Unless a library's activities can be marshalled into some kind of support structure with accompanying values, it will be difficult to determine transaction costs or to demonstrate the community value of library activities.

FIGURE 5.2   Organizing for Effectiveness

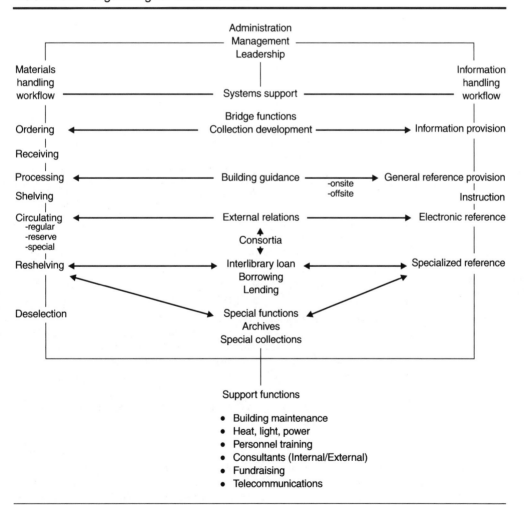

Summary

Library budget preparation must take into account all information alternatives, remembering that the costs associated with each alternative may be very variable indeed and may reach across budget categories. Over time it may also be possible to replace existing paper collections with microform or electronic versions, and attention should always be paid to the possibilities of cooperative resource retention and sharing. Nevertheless librarians will have to continue to make decisions based on local needs. Some alternatives, such as database access, carry with them staff and other service costs, and librarians will have to decide whether these costs will be absorbed or passed on. Moreover, electronic information sources require added expenditure for equipment, electricity, and similar operational costs. Only too often this kind of budgetary need is overlooked. It is not simply a matter of deciding what percentage of the library materials budget should be directed to nonprint media, but rather one of rethinking the library's service and, consequently, budget response to user needs. All media have a role to play in providing library service, and it is far too soon to base future budgets on the idea that print is outmoded.

Notes

1. Charles T. Meadow, "On the Future of the Book, or Does It Have a Future?" *Journal of Scholarly Publishing* 26, no. 4 (July 1995): 187–96.

2. Tom Clark, "On the Cost Differences between Publishing a Book in Paper and in the Electronic Medium," *Library Resources & Technical Services* 39, no. 1 (January 1995): 23–28; and Brett Fairbairn, "The Present and Future of Historical Journals," *Journal of Scholarly Publishing* 27, no. 2 (January 1996): 59–74, both examine the problems faced by such publications in going electronic.

3. Here one might consider the recent series of editorials in *Choice* regarding the problems faced by publishers in deciding what to publish and in what quantity.

4. Clifford Lynch, "Pricing Electronic Reference Works: The Dilemma of the Mixed Library and Consumer Marketplace," in *Issues in Collection Management: Librarians, Booksellers, Publishers,* ed. Murray S. Martin (Greenwich, Conn.: JAI Press, 1995) 19–34.

5. Murray S. Martin, "Is Your Library Reference Poor?" (*Technicalities* 16, no. 1 (January 1996): 5–7; and 16, no. 2 (February 1996): 1, 5–7).

6. U.S. Department of Education, National Center for Education Statistics, *NAEP Trends in Academic Progress: Science, Mathematics, Reading, Writing* (Washington, D.C., 1993); *Executive Summary of the NAEP 1992 Reading Report Card for the Nation and the States* (Washington, D.C., 1993).

7. The Somers (Connecticut) Public Library abandoned its FirstSearch telephone number database in favor of a CD-ROM system. In comments to *The Hartford Courant,* Marlene Melcher of the Hartford Public Library said, "You can't beat the accuracy of phone books" (May 28, 1996: B1, B4). The problem, of course, is that they use up a great deal of space. It is also necessary to remember that almost all such listings are to some extent out-of-date before they are published. This is not confined to printed media. Conversation at the American Library Association meeting in New York in 1996 made it clear that as many as 25 percent of e-mail addresses in any directory can be wrong, a feeling confirmed by the

authors when trying to contact other librarians, with an almost 100 percent failure rate based on using existing information.

8. "Academic Libraries Solving Journal Cancellation Woes," *Library Journal* 122, no. 12 (July 1997): 125.

9. Eleanor B. Gossen and Suzanne Irving, "Ownership Versus Access and Low-Use Periodical Titles," *Library Resources & Technical Services* 29, no. 1 (January 1995): 43–52.

10. Ross Atkinson, "Access, Ownership, and the Future of Collection Development," in *Collection Management and Development: Issues in an Electronic Era,* ed. Peggy Johnson and Bonnie MacEwan (Chicago: American Library Association, 1994) 92–109.

11. See Carol Tenopir's column "Online Databases" in *Library Journal* for continuing updates on these and other issues.

12. Many New Zealand census records relating to women's issues are now published by Daphne Brazzell, Ltd. Although technically this is a joint publishing venture with the Government Printer, the publications must be purchased in the same way as regular trade books.

13. The Information Access Company conducted a survey of 880 libraries and discovered a substantial growth in site licensing, including a doubling of such arrangements by public libraries. At the same time expenditure on CD-ROMs grew by 5 percent as reported in *Bottom Line* 9, no. 1 (1996): 48.

14. Public Library Association. Public Policy for Public Libraries Section. Fee-Based Services Committee. *Position Paper on Fee-Based Services* (Chicago: PLA, 1996). See also the ongoing activities of the Fee-Based Services in Academic Libraries Discussion Group and their publication *FISCAL Notes.*

15. Michael Wooliscroft, "Access and Ownership: Academic Libraries, Collecting and Service Responsibilities, and the Emerging Benefits of Electronic-Publishing and Document Supply," *New Zealand Libraries* 47, no. 9 (March 1994): 170–80.

16. William J. Baumol and Sue Ann Batey Blackman, "Electronics, the Cost Disease, and the Operation of Libraries," *Journal of the American Society of Information Science* 34, no. 4 (1983): 181–91.

6
Purchase Alternatives

In the days when the only consideration was whether or not to purchase a book or other publication, the resolution was relatively simple. It either fitted into the library's sphere of interest and its budget or it did not. Now that there are several other alternatives to buying, the chain of decision is somewhat longer. Matters to consider now include:

- First, is it an essential purchase?
- Second, what format should be considered?
- Third, can it be leased or borrowed?
- Fourth, what about access to online sources?
- Fifth, is it a library or an individual responsibility?

When these questions have been asked and answered, the library must then decide on its mode of implementation.

Primary Concerns

Essential purchases are relatively simple. Whether print or other format, if an item is for sale, the library simply sends out a purchase order, pays the resulting bill, and the item then becomes library property. Variations result from publication exchanges, the pursuit of free publications, and the deposit of government publications, but these do not change the relationship between the library, the supplier, and the user. One useful intermediary service developed by consortia or state libraries has been to arrange discount plans with library dealers and vendors. These may also be linked with centralized ordering and processing.

Because certain publications, such as databases, are often beyond the budgetary scope of any single library, a second mode of acquisition comes into play—leasing, or paying for access.

Here the library has to consider the form of the contract involved.

- Is it simply payment for actual uses made, or is it a contract for service?
- What are the conditions that go with the transaction?

Whereas the purchase of a book ended the transaction, a contract for service may involve annual payments and/or payments per use. There may be conditions attached to downloading, adding to a local network, or offprinting the results of searches. There can also be limits on who can use the information contained in the database.

At present, the Internet (and similar networks) appear to be free, since the bulk of the operating cost is picked up by the federal government.[1] Similarly, universities and similar institutions may pay for the general operating costs, leaving only access and user costs to be paid for by the library. Public and school libraries, however, may find that even if the initial access costs are underwritten by federal or state subsidies, the later operating costs will fall squarely on the library budget. This issue has not yet been fully addressed by any of the constituencies involved, even while such update needs are becoming a major concern for business and industry (for example, the Year 2000 Syndrome) and the need to remain competitive in a rapidly changing universe. It would seem that at some future time the costs of replacing both hardware and software will fall squarely on the institutional budget. All the philanthropy of a Bill Gates cannot change this situation.[2] Public libraries are especially vulnerable to such costs, since they need to be paid for by taxes, which, in turn, need to be solicited. For special libraries, the costs may be part of the cost of doing business, but will almost certainly be recovered from clients or other internal operational units. These differences will result in differences in the approaches taken by the library in question. It is possible, however, that, just as many universities and colleges learned the necessity of passing on telephone costs to the various budget units to ensure accountability, they may soon decide to pass on Internet costs. This will certainly happen if the various proposals concerning fees for access are implemented.[3] No institution can afford to allow runaway costs into budget planning. Some have already decided that they cannot pay all the costs, for example, of off-campus access to the Internet, and it may well be that further such decisions are likely.

Purchase on Demand

The phrase "purchase on demand" has been used from time to time, meaning that libraries will buy materials only when they are specifically requested.[4] This can mean that a paperback will be bought and given to the requester because it is simpler than going through the whole process of cataloging when it is likely to be needed only by the requester. Or, it can mean that the library will wait and see whether it is possible to buy at a discounted price, e.g., after a paperback edition has been brought out and the hardback edition is available at a lower price. Now, with the emergence of document delivery, it can also mean that the document required will be purchased and the requester will be asked to pay for it.

This kind of process cannot apply to serials and similar continuing publications, except at the article level. Even the hardiest budgets cannot provide the funds to support individual needs in this manner, so it is more likely to be a matter of "just in time" rather than "just in case," meaning that the library cannot afford to purchase materials only in the hope that they will be used. This alternative was presented by Fred Lynden at the Charleston Conference on Acquisitions in 1995, when he stressed that it was necessary to consider user needs as the primary guideline rather than aim at all-purpose collections. This does not mean that libraries should not continue to specialize where appropriate, but that they can no longer hope to be all-inclusive. One side-effect of "just-in-time" acquisitions is likely to be an increase in rush ordering and rush processing, which adds to library costs. These kinds of orders will most likely lie outside the range of regular ordering arrangements, because there is always a time element, which requires direct contact with publishers rather than with vendors, usually a difficult and time-consuming process. Some limits may have to be placed because library customers can easily learn that by delaying their orders they can achieve speedier results. A surcharge may well be appropriate when it is a question of special service.

Collecting Profiles

The development of a collecting profile has long been necessary even for small institutions. The actual needs will vary with the kind of institution. Too many guidelines in the past have looked first at size and then developed financial requirements. The first step is to look at the actual mission of the institution. Some of the measures that might be used are shown below.

Institutional Mission

Academic
   Teaching
   Research
   Public Service

Public
   Literacy
   Information
   Community Outreach
   Leisure Reading

Special
   Research
   Support
   Information

School
    Literacy
    Learning
    Support

Then it is necessary to look at the policies that derive from the mission statement. These policies should address the definition of the collection, the development of that collection, and its maintenance.

Collection definition
    Quality
    Quantity
    Distribution
    Location
    Access/Ownership
Collection development
    Purchases
    Gifts and exchanges
    Sharing
    Renting/Leasing
    Alternative formats
Collection maintenance
    Retention
    Retirement
    Preservation
    Storage/Location

Only when this has been done is it possible to assign the proper roles to purchase, access, and information retrieval. This requires a careful assessment of user needs and library capacity, since both must be kept in balance. The results may well differ by kind of library, but are almost certain to require a reconsideration of the library's collection development program.

What Is Appropriate?

What lies within the institution's interests and what does not can often be a thorny problem, especially with regard to reference purchases. These may as often help users in uncovering resources the library does not own as they may assist users in exploiting owned resources. If the goal is to assist users in finding resources to solve their needs, the library will have to provide reference resources outside its nominal sphere of interest. The personal interests of faculty or other users may lie totally outside library goals, but providing information can still assist in furthering institutional goals. Purchasing materials to forward these interests does not mesh with institutional priorities, so libraries will have to look at alternative means of answering such needs. Examining these needs can lead to the further refining of library purchasing profiles, and to determinations as to what alternatives are the most likely to meet user needs. This process can become very complex, when it is realized that special interests may be quite temporary in institutional terms. For instance, after a specific research project has been concluded, nobody in the institution may be interested any longer in the materials accumulated to meet that need.

Issues that should be considered are:

- Is the subject matter of primary importance to the library?
- Is the actual publication likely to be of lasting importance to the library?
- Is the need temporary or longer lasting; i.e., will there be further users?
- Are there alternatives to purchasing that will meet the need?
- Can the library afford the cost of purchasing the material in question?

While purchasing books, periodicals, and electronic sources remains the best way to satisfy major local needs, libraries have to consider whether there are other ways of meeting them. The basic question is whether they are ongoing or temporary. Continuing needs are best met by purchasing materials, since multiple uses lower the cost per use. If the need is temporary or discontinuous, interlibrary loan, purchase on demand, or document delivery may be the best answer. Before automation, libraries had little guidance as to whether specific needs were one-time or continuing. The records of use generated by automated circulation systems, and the various programs designed to record interlibrary loan usage, can help in determining whether the materials in question are needed on a long-term basis or only sporadically.

Alternatives

The primary alternatives are purchasing and borrowing. The latter may be attained through interlibrary loan, document delivery, database use, or via electronic networks.

- Purchasing is relatively straightforward, the others less so.
- Interlibrary loan involves a sequence of expensive activities, whose costs may or may not be recovered.
- Document delivery involves substantial costs, both in terms of library activity and actual charges.

- Databases can provide seemingly miraculous responses to individual needs but also cost substantial sums of money, whether for direct use or for the transmission of information.
- Electronic networks seem "free," but conceal substantial overhead costs, in staff time, transmission, and/or downloading and printing charges.

Within this range of possibilities, purchase still remains the primary mode for library acquisition of materials, where those materials are likely to be of interest to numerous users on a continuing basis. This is true especially for the reference materials instanced earlier, even though they do not generate lending records to justify their purchase. This fact is, incidentally, a prime reason for seeing that in-house uses are properly counted, since that will give some idea of whether noncirculating collections are used and needed.

Consortial and Access Relationships

While libraries will mostly continue to buy materials independently to meet their users' needs, there is an increasing trend toward buying within a consortial framework. An example of such a relationship is described in Rodney Erickson's article on *Choice*-based acquisition.[5] While no one would suggest that this is a way of replacing individual library-based acquisition programs, it offers a significant level of improvement over independent selection choices at a time when library budgets are strained to meet even the most basic needs. Other alternatives are looking at the areas where the members of a consortium provide unique resources and adapting acquisition programs to incorporate this knowledge. In reverse, the same applies to serial cancellation projects, although there is little evidence that there have been many attempts to handle such cancellations collectively.[6] In fact, most libraries have proceeded alone, without looking at what other libraries are doing. Admittedly there are difficulties in working out ways in which to coordinate cancellations, but the long-term difficulties resulting from not having done so may be much greater, as individual library users seek to find materials they need. Many questions regarding the use of and need for cancelled subscriptions have emerged. Some studies suggest that prestige, rather than actual need, requires the retention of expensive journals of record. As reported by Charles Hamaker and others, postcancellation needs turned out to be rather less than expected, and could well be handled within interlibrary loan and document delivery guidelines.[7]

To a large degree, the actions undertaken by an individual library will reflect the ways in which it cooperates with other libraries. Where there is a close relationship, each library will consider the effects of its policy changes on the cooperative. Where the relationships are looser, each library will tend to follow its own path, regardless of the consequences for the group. The future financial setting seems to suggest that librarians would be well advised to look carefully at the benefits accruing from cooperative activity and to seek ways in which to meld them into their collection strategies.

Legal and Economic Implications

It has not been usual for librarians to think about the legal implications of their actions in purchasing library materials. Apart from the occasional copyright problem, the ownership of printed materials seemed to settle the matter. The library owned the materials that had been purchased and was able to lend them to users or to other libraries without added cost. There are some exceptions to this rule, as in countries where there is a Public Lending Right which generates income for authors based on library circulation of their titles, but, by and large, libraries have been able to lend without restrictions.

Interestingly, the same rule applies to the purchase of secondhand materials. While we might think of this mostly in relation to antiquarian purchases, it was the basis on which the Universal Serials and Book Exchange (USBE) conducted and still conducts its business of supplying libraries with periodical issues.[8] Unlike articles sought through document delivery, these sales are not subject to royalty payments and it can well be cheaper to purchase an entire issue from USBE than to seek one article via document delivery. In the same way it is usually more prudent to subscribe to a relatively cheap serial than to pay royalties on several articles a year.

With the advent of electronic publishing, where ownership may well be uncertain and even access may result in a fee, the importance of ownership has gained new meaning. Electronic publications do not exist in a tangible format that can be picked up and moved. Using them involves software and hardware, often supplied by the "publisher," and can be subject to a wide variety of rules and charges. Most such purchases are governed by contract law. In fact, they may not even be purchases but leases. These "nit-picking" differences may well become all-important in the twenty-first century.

Contracts

There are also variations in what is supplied under the contract. CD-ROMs are usually purchased outright, but, where there is an update service, they can more nearly resemble serials. Some are provided for use on the library's own hardware; others come with their own hardware and form a separate user station. It is always important to look closely at the rules surrounding their use, which may sometimes prevent use by corporations or for commercial purposes. In some cases libraries are required to return superseded discs, and may be required to return any still in their possession if they cease to use the service. To a certain degree, this can be justified in terms of preventing either piracy or reliance on out-of-date information, but it leaves in doubt the library's actual ownership. Special rules may apply to artistic products, such as records, videos, compact discs, or collections of images of paintings, where copying may be prohibited unless a performance fee is paid. This has serious implications for the original, which may no longer be available for repurchase, even though the library's copy is no longer usable. It also prevents the taping (or other recording) of performances except for classroom use under stringent conditions. Libraries cannot accept and retain such copies, something often forgotten by academics.

Databases

Databases present further variations. Few librarians are in position of being able to buy many of these, and choose to access them, either on their own, through joint purchase by a consortium, or by using the services of an information vendor. These purchases are subject to contract law, largely because they are not subject to copyright. There may also be provision for an annual use fee as well as intitial purchase cost, or restrictions may be placed on who can use the database. It may be possible to buy a certain number of searches, e.g., as with OCLC's FirstSearch, and provide these to library users either free or for a fee. Others services, such as UnCover Inc., cannot be purchased, but provide the possibility of purchasing on demand articles wanted by a user, though the costs involved can be substantial. Here the library also has to determine what out-of-pocket costs will be recovered and whether to recover staff costs as well. Much of a library's use will be determined by the kind of database in question: citations only, abstracts, or full text. The first two imply further action to obtain the needed text, even when it is available within the library's collections, and here it is worthwhile to determine whether it is possible for the vendor to index the library's own holdings, which could increase in-house use, cheaper than seeking outside supply. Full-text retrieval may also involve substantial costs in downloading and printing. In any event, the library will have to pay (or recover) the costs involved in the search and recovery process.

Electronic Publications

The status of electronic publications within this spectrum is not yet clear. Much information on the Internet is in the public domain. In other cases the author(s) may make specific allowance for copying or may impose restrictions. Electronic journals may be subject to a subscription fee. There are few "books," so far, because publishers are still uncertain about how to reclaim their costs without an elaborate system of encryption and fees. This may change if Congress decides to exclude electronic materials from "fair use," allowing publishers to charge a fee simply for browsing. The enforcement of any such rules may be very difficult, but they would be certain to add to libraries' problems.

It seems somewhat far-fetched to make libraries responsible for what their users do with the Internet, though this is clearly at issue until legal challenges to the recent law providing penalties for providing juvenile access to pornographic materials have been settled.[9] Although the Supreme Court decision in favor of free access may seem to have settled this issue, state and local laws and challenges are likely to continue for some time. This kind of issue can be expected to continue until laws based on the printed medium have been adjusted to the requirements of the electronic medium. The whole picture is complicated by its international nature. The French government has been trying to impose French translation on any electronic publications within France, but has so far had little success. This may seem a little silly but shows the kinds of problems that Internet access raises. The international nature of information is becoming increasingly important and may well have great impact on its format, its costs, and its distribution, especially if it becomes necessary to provide multiple language versions, or there are several national standards.

Economic Side Effects

The economic implications of changes in publishing formats have not yet been subject to extensive study, but it is already clear that libraries are diverting more and more of their "materials" budgets to electronic and other nonprint publications. The *Against the Grain (ATG)* Annual Report Survey for 1996, for example, reported that 17 percent of the materials budget was for electronic materials.[10] Such decisions carry with them a number of budget implications that are not confined to the library materials budget.

Whereas purchasing a book implied little other than processing, shelving, and circulation costs, significant in total though they are, purchasing nonprint and especially electronic materials implies the addition of equipment, supplies, reuse and redesign of library space, maintenance costs, power and telecommunications costs, staff and user training, and the costs of downloading or printing needed materials. Because the latter are not readily reusable by another patron, they become personal rather than community services and libraries may well feel justified in passing those costs on to the individual user, although this has been a hotly disputed move.[11] Doing so makes significant changes in the library's budgetary base, since certain services become almost self-supporting and have to be regarded as separate programs, in much the same way as photocopying, which is now generally on an independent footing and not part of the general budget request. Even without the issue of cost recovery, the shift of expenditure from print to electronics will change the proportions allocated to various kinds of publications. The "access" provided by CD-ROMs, databases, etc., will decrease the proportions assigned to regularly purchased print materials unless there are major increases in the budget.[12] Whether this will affect periodicals and serials more than monographs is still moot, but, while most electronic publications are serial or serial-based, it would seem likely that the serial portion of the materials budget will decrease. Increases in document delivery will probably have the same effect. The combination of these factors may also affect publishing decisions both as to books and to periodicals.[13] Libraries may well find themselves diverting more staff and other resources to borrowing and other means of document retrieval.

Summary

Purchasing library materials for indefinite retention sounds like a relatively clear notion. But, when "purchases" come to include electronic materials the library does not "own," it is clear that other considerations must be taken into account when setting up a budget. The production of books and other materials happens within a very complex web of relationships.

- If libraries move toward the electronic versions, what will happen to the needs and expectations of individual purchasers?
- What are the differences between library purchase, lease, and purchase on demand for an individual user?

Cooperative programs may work better within the regular world of publications than within the world of online access, but in any situation the library must still keep in mind the needs of its users and how best they can be served. All librarians need to remain aware that alternatives to purchase have differing effects on the budget, depending on how labor or equipment intensive they are. The balancing of these different needs is the single most important factor in the new library budget. The interreactions of library, user, publisher, and vendor are now much more complicated and have broader effects. Only close examination of these effects can enable librarians to set up a truly responsive budget.

Notes

1. *Intellectual Property and the National Information Infrastructure: The Report of the Working Group on Intellectual Property Rights.* Bruce A. Lehman, Chair (Washington, D.C.: U.S. Department of Commerce, 1995).

2. Murray S. Martin, columns in *Technicalities* and *The Bottom Line.*

3. *Intellectual Property* . . . . There are several references to the matter of charges but few of any substance. The underlying suggestion is that the issues can be resolved by agreement between the various partners to a transaction. So far, this agreement on charges and payments has not been achieved, except in a few instances, nor has the matter of "fair use" of electronic materials, despite the continuing intergroup discussion.

4. Fred Lynden, in a paper presented to the Charleston conference in 1995.

5. Rodney Erickson, "*Choice* for Collection Development," *Library Acquisitions: Practice and Theory* 16, no. 1 (1992): 43–49.

6. Tina E. Chrzatowski and Karen A. Schmidt, "Surveying the Damage: Academic Library Serial Cancellations 1987–88 through 1989–90," *College & Research Libraries* 54, no. 2 (March 1993): 92–102.

7. Jane P. Kleiner and Charles A. Hamaker, "Libraries 2000: Transforming Libraries Using Document Delivery, Needs Assessment, and Networked Resources," *College & Research Libraries* 58, no. 4 (July 1997): 355–74; along with other information presented at the ALCTS Preconference, "The Business of Acquisitions," San Francisco, 1997.

8. The position of the renewed USBE has been ably presented in a series of news releases. Information can be obtained from USBE: United States Book Exchange, 2969 West 25th Street, Cleveland, OH 44113-5332.

9. There are numerous notes and articles on "pornography" and the problems faced by libraries when providing access to the Internet. This has reached the public media, as witness *The Hartford Courant*'s article "Facing Up to Cyberporn" (April 25, 1996, 14–17). In the same issue "A Lesson in Race Relations," by John Perritano, pointed out that there are other concerns, and that public authorities can easily bypass their duty to examine serious local problems. (p. 7)

10. "*Against the Grain* Annual Report Survey," *Against the Grain* 9, no. 1 (February 1997): 16. The actual figures are 7 percent for online resources and gateways, 4 percent for electronic serials, 4 percent for CD-ROMs, and 2 percent for other electronic materials.

11. Public Library Association, Public Policy for Public Libraries Section. Fee-Based Services Committee. *Position Paper on Fee-Based Services* (Chicago: PLA, 1996).

12. Murray S. Martin, "The Invasion of the Library Materials Budget by Technology. Serials and Databases: Buying More with Less?" *Serials Review* 18, no. 3 (1992): 7–17.

13. Brett Fairbairn, "The Present and Future of Historical Journals," *Journal of Scholarly Publishing* 27, no. 2 (January 1996): 59–74.

7

Interlibrary Loan

For many years, interlibrary loan (ILL) has been seen as the standard response to a library's inability to provide ready access to all the information needed by library users. When the materials needed were not available in the local library, they were sought from another library. This was a perfectly reasonable response in a setting where the exchange of information resources between libraries involved a wide range of collection and bibliographic knowledge. By and large, it was conducted without too many rules, conventions, and financial concerns, though libraries did develop a fairly stringent set of guidelines about what could and could not be borrowed. These guidelines addressed mostly local concerns about individual library needs, such as reference, reserve, and internal priorities.[1] Its success depended on the bibliographic and navigational skills developed by librarians well versed in the use of such tools as the *National Union Catalog* and other regional union catalogs, the various bibliographic tools listing the ownership of periodicals and newspapers, e.g., the *Union List of Serials* and the *Union List of Newspapers,* and simply a knowledge of library specialties. Although this may seem like a serendipitous coming together of disparate sets of knowledge, it was a finely honed, sophisticated, professional procedure. It is, moreover, a primary example of the value of personal knowledge within any institution. Because there were limits to what could be accomplished by these methods, growth was relatively slow and did not require a large proportion of the library's budget.

Winds of Change

As the bibliographic utilities began to expand and became more sophisticated, for example OCLC and RLIN, it seemed as if it would be possible to "clericalize" interlibrary loan, since these tools would make it clear what was where. After all, if the wanted material showed up on OCLC, what further direction was needed? The utilities themselves began developing more and more sophisticated communications and delivery systems, for example the OCLC FirstSearch and Interlibrary Loan modules or RLIN's Ariel. The result of these changes has been a rapid growth in the amount of interlibrary loan demand, which has often outstripped the libraries' ability to perform. The statistics provided by OCLC suggest that the present rate of interlibrary loan requests is somewhat more than a million per month, a rapidly rising proportion of total library transactions. However, the concept of "clerical-ization" is somewhat simplistic because interlibrary loan exists within a complex world of legal, commercial, contractual, and pragmatic rules, not all of which are easily handled by any employee at whatever level. If librarians wish to provide the best possible service to their users, they will need to look carefully at the ways they invest in their services.

Legal Issues

The legal Doctrine of Fair Use regulates the way in which libraries can copy and lend existing materials without breaching copyright. The Doctrine of First Sale determines their right to lend already purchased materials. Sub-sidiary issues relate to the replacement of pages lost or stolen from pur-chased materials.

Many of these activities are subject to guidelines prepared by the Com-mission on New Technological Uses (CONTU), which determine how much a library may borrow; others relate only to the fact that the library is not substituting borrowing for buying. There are still many legal uncertainties surrounding copying within institutions (the Texaco case, which was settled out of court, related to the ways in which libraries could make copies for branches or distant participants), and the degree to which libraries can use copied materials to satisfy disparate requests. The range of legal decisions surrounding these transactions has not made the life of the interlibrary loan librarian any easier, nor the fact that, internationally, there can be explicit and implicit differences between countries in the application of copyright law. This has not been addressed by the various committees looking at Internet access. The differences between national copyright codes can make the life of the interlibrary loan staff much more difficult.

When to Borrow?

Nevertheless, it has become accepted that there are many situations in which a library is justified in seeking to borrow materials for local use or in seeking photocopies of specific articles. Doing so calls into play a significant portion of the library's operating expenditures. There have been many studies of the cost of interlibrary loan.[2] Even while admitting the validity of these studies, conducted mostly among larger libraries, the question must be raised of what alternatives are available if user needs are to be met. Pur-chasing and processing new materials is even more expensive, supposing that the materials in question could be purchased. Document delivery (to be considered in chapter 8) has extensive cost considerations and questions as to achievement. Shared access programs may act as a substitute, but are not readily available to all libraries, particularly those in isolated settings. An interesting study of the comparative costs of subscribing to periodicals or borrowing articles is presented by Bruce R. Kingma in chapter 7 of *The Economics of Access versus Ownership,* which sets out studies conducted at the University of Albany.[3] The results provide some interesting paradigms. Librarians need to think carefully through the various response modes of purchase and access before making facile decisions.

Always having regard to legal restrictions, as, for example, the number of articles from a specific periodical that can be borrowed, the fact remains that most libraries will find that their local acquisitions budgets are unequal to the task of purchasing all the materials that library users may want. An example of an unexpected result from new technology is the increased use of interlibrary loan by undergraduates, resulting from their use of online databases.[4] The consideration of interlibrary loan and its alternatives thus becomes an integral part of planning the resource or access budget. Libraries, generally, have not followed this method of budgeting, despite the clear evidence that they need to look more closely at the alternatives available to them. For the most part, they have maintained traditional proportions and traditional programs, or have responded to budget pressure by doing away with specific activities.

Costs

Any interlibrary loan transaction carries with it significant budgetary costs including staff, equipment, and other operational expenditures.[5] While these costs may not be exactly the same for special, public, and school libraries, they are significant in terms of satisfying user needs. How far any library can go in providing such services without attempting to recover some or all of the costs is still a matter of debate. It has even been suggested that interlibrary loan should be thought of as a direct personal service and should therefore be subject to full cost recovery. Certainly many libraries are imposing fees or cost recovery charges, but for the most part ILL is seen as a substitute for purchase or a replacement service for a library failure.

Borrowing

The basic premise behind interlibrary loan has been that the library is remedying a defect in its own supply system and, therefore, the user should not be penalized by paying, as it were, a second time. There may also be deeper implications and effects on the library's acquisition program since librarians have to decide when to buy and when to borrow.[6] It is, moreover, a mutual system between libraries, not between libraries and users, because the costs and benefits tend to cancel one another out in institutional rather than personal terms.

The premise of free service has come under close examination at a time when all libraries must examine closely their costs and their services. The basic issue is what libraries should provide free and what they should charge back when it is a question of individual rather than community benefits. When an individual transaction can run to $20 or $30, it has to be asked whether there should be some element of cost recovery. It would seem that libraries are now tending toward a larger degree of cost recovery, whether from individual users or from other libraries.

The direct benefit from an interlibrary loan transaction enures to the individual user but there may be diffuse benefits for the community as well—a completed research project, better industrial or business procedures, a better student project, or simply a better informed citizen. The complex role of information in the improvement of personal, commercial, or public activities has hardly begun to be considered, though there are signs the business community is beginning to see the need for and the benefits of knowledge as the basis for their success.[7] Libraries need to demonstrate more clearly what they can contribute to the process,[8] including the accumulated knowledge possessed by their staffs.

While it may seem that the vast improvements in bibliographic and locational access have simplified interlibrary loan to the degree that it has become a straightforward clerical transaction, it is *vital* to remember even the most sophisticated and extensive bibliographic services currently available do not, and will not, for the foreseeable future, cover all the types of materials likely to be requested. The various commercial document delivery services do not even begin to cover the entire range of the information that exists and are, moreover, geared to that which is most readily available and commercially profitable. The obscure or noncommercial publications that are available only from limited sources cannot be readily accessed by commercial services and will remain the province of interlibrary loan. Moreover, the borrowing and lending of monographs as permitted under copyright laws is quite outside the scope of document delivery, and there is always the question of government publications which are not copyrighted, at least in the United States.

Libraries will have to continue, for some time to come, to include interlibrary borrowing within their options for information delivery. This does not imply a totally cost-free service, only that such transactions must be included within any budgetary strategy. The same is true for borrowing via ILL, and libraries will also have to determine what kinds of charges to pass on, if any.

Lending

Lending is the obverse of borrowing. The one could not take place without the other. Indeed, in New Zealand, it is expected that libraries participating in Interloan will strive to seek a balance between borrowing and lending.[9] This fact is recognized in the extensive agreements, formal or informal, between libraries concerning interlibrary loan. It is possible for any one library to belong to many consortia or groups, or to participate in state and regionally sponsored schemes. Within such plans, there are usually agreements about cost recovery and charges. Charges may also be prohibited, or a state may provide a subsidy to participating libraries to ensure the continuance of the service. These variations make it almost impossible to provide any definitive ground rules either for levying charges or for providing free service. Each library must look carefully at the conditions surrounding its use of interlibrary loan and make financial decisions based on those conditions.

The cost studies referred to earlier make it clear that the cost to the lending library can be almost as great as the cost to the borrowing library. Moreover, with the rapid expansion of bibliographic utility records it is now possible to find out very quickly what libraries hold the needed materials, especially those who catalog their additions promptly. This can affect even small libraries in an area where other libraries are not as prompt. A situation that recently came to the attention of the author involved a library's lending operation that was growing more swiftly than its borrowing, largely because its bibliographic records were more complete. This may seem unique, but many libraries do not submit their new acquisition records to shared databases on a regular basis, largely because they cannot afford the cost, particularly for ephemeral materials.

Many libraries have decided they must charge for lending because of the associated costs.[10] These charges may include a general fee, the cost of recovering the publication, postage, and/or photocopy costs.

- The general fee may be a deterrent to casual enquiries, or simply one based on internal costs.
- In large libraries with several branches, finding a publication can be a time-consuming process, and some libraries have decided to incorporate a recovery fee.
- Photocopying or microfilming is an added expense, which most libraries feel justified in charging back to the borrower. The cost may be a set fee, or adjusted to the amount of material copied.
- Charges may be waived for members of a consortium or a regional network.

Borrowing libraries need to be aware of the charges, which can be found in several directories, though all have to realize that they may have changed since publication.[11] Most such charges are applied more often to articles than to books. Borrowing libraries have to decide whether to recover these costs from users or to absorb any or all charges.

Lending and Borrowing Policies

Local library lending policies and charges should be spelled out clearly, so that would-be borrowers can determine whether or not to proceed. As with all collection policies, any decisions on cost recovery will affect the library's budget. The intent may be to fund in part the interlibrary loan operation, in which case the income can be seen as offsetting the cost. Charges can be meant to limit the amount of lending the library will provide but may well be modified in accordance with any consortial arrangements. In any event, these decisions will affect the ways in which the library handles the mutual sharing of information. Too stringent a level of charges may make it difficult for the library to recover materials wanted by its own users; too low a level may strain the library's resources.

Photocopying

In many instances the best response to a request is not the dispatch of the entire publication but sending a photocopy of the required material. Here, however, we run into the problems of copyright.

- What is allowable?
- What is impossible?

The problem is not so much the individual request as it is the cumulative number of requests that relate to the same publication. There are differences associated with classroom use and individual use. There is also the matter of what is subject to copyright laws and what is exempt. These issues may not be entirely clear until after extensive consultation with the prospective user. A further complication relates to the proportion of the original publication that is being requested and how it will be used. While it may be possible to copy an entire publication for personal use, it is seldom possible to reproduce and distribute an entire work (poem, diagram, etc.). Understanding these differences can make it much simpler to make decisions about what can or cannot be done. In many cases, the intention is to produce a further work for students from copies of other sources. Interlibrary loan is not intended to support such activities. Anyone seeking to produce such a work must seek copyright permissions before beginning publication.

Library Initiation

It is most usual for a library to initiate an interlibrary loan request. The very name suggests that this is a transaction between libraries. Now, however, the accessibility of the Internet and similar protocols has made it relatively easy for the individual user to bypass the library. Many would say this represents better user service, but also have to realize that many users, without significant bibliographic expertise, will ask for materials that are readily available in their own libraries. They may also choose holding libraries that impose significant charges for requests, even though other sources are available.

For these reasons, it is still a valid protocol to ask that would-be borrowers check with the local interlibrary loan service before initiating a request. It is also possible, thanks to the many software programs available, for librarians to inspect customer-initiated requests before they are transmitted to other libraries.

The rationale for library origination is that the library is in a better position to check the bibliographic and locational information of the request. There may be special protocols associated with cooperating libraries, provision for free photocopy, or similar special terms that make it highly desirable to use a specific library. The library is also in a better position to know whether there are mutual agreements about photocopy or document delivery. Most libraries operate within a complex network of agreements concerning the sharing of information, some of which assure access to otherwise inaccessible collections or may reduce the costs of borrowing. While it may seem reasonable simply to choose the first library on a list of holding libraries, the associated costs may make other decisions more appropriate. Such decisions can have a major effect on the costs of interlibrary loan, hence the importance of staff involvement.

Customer Initiation

It is becoming more common for library users to be able to initiate their own interlibrary loan requests—though this is more likely to relate to document delivery than to traditional interlibrary loan. The idea is that customer initiation can save the library money. If the customer can manage to complete flawlessly all the needed protocols, that could be true. For the most part, however, the library still needs to run the request past a scanning program to ensure that it is not for something owned by the library or for something that is unlikely to be provided via interlibrary loan; e.g., reference materials or current popular titles.

If a library decides that customer initiation of interlibrary loan requests is desirable, it will need to set up appropriate protocols to ensure that legal and cooperative agreements are being followed. It will also need to determine what limits, if any, will be placed on use and what kinds of cost recovery mechanisms can be used, e.g., credit cards. The "customer" may not always understand these mechanisms and may seek to circumvent them. These controls may seem to be institutional restraints but are essential if good relationships with other libraries are to be maintained.

The objective of customer-initiated ILL may be to reduce the library costs associated with such transactions, but it is important to realize that the costs of repairing damaged library relationships or recovering "lost" materials may outweigh the apparent user benefits. Unless the library is prepared to provide extensive user education, it must be willing to pick up the costs that result from abuses of the interlibrary loan system. These may include overdue returns, mutilation, and theft.

Legal Issues

Clearly, the most significant legal issue in interlibrary loan is copyright. There is an extensive literature relating to this question,[12] but there are few definitive answers. Copyright law is under intensive review around the world and, until the various governments have determined their positions, there will still be room for the exercise of judgment. Australia, Canada, and New Zealand are slowly working toward the resolution of many difficulties. All librarians need to be aware that decisions elsewhere may affect materially what they can actually do. In the United States, the judicial process is slowly working toward the resolution of many difficulties. Many out-of-court settlements have made final determination of outstanding issues problematic, because there were no court decisions on the issues. There is, moreover, the still uncertain status of electronic publications, where it is possible that the publisher, rather than the author, may set the standard for use and for charges.[13] If it is finally determined that any consultation of an electronic publication is similar to a performance, the entire system of consultation, reading, and lending of publications will change radically. Congress is also considering a proposal to extend the term of copyright from life plus 50 years to life plus 70 years, and libraries are seeking to find some relief for their use of such protected materials beyond the earlier period. Internationally, many countries are trying to bring their copyright legislation in line with the latest international agreements on trade and tariffs.[14] This continuing change in the legal and commercial environment means that interlibrary loan will become increasingly complicated. Libraries need to be aware of this legal context as they attempt to redirect their policies regarding acquisition and access.

Despite this, libraries are likely to continue to realize that it is possible to meet some of their users' needs only through such shared programs as interlibrary loan—particularly for international publications which are seldom readily available either online or from commercial services—which must, therefore, be regarded as a continuing part of their resource budgets.

Summary

Interlibrary loan is likely to remain an integral part of libraries' information services for the foreseeable future. Its role may, however, change, as libraries take into account the new methods of information delivery. There will be differences between what can be accomplished by document delivery services or databases and by the traditional sharing of printed resources. These differences have not yet been adequately defined.

The cost differentials between differing information service patterns have not yet been fully explored. What is appropriate in one setting may be inappropriate in another. A library must take into account such differences in setting up its budget. Borrowing from another library makes sense when the original library is unable to obtain or purchase the wanted item. It may also be the only possible way when it is a matter of a scarce printed item. The process becomes a little more indistinct when it relates to obtaining photocopied articles or parts of a publication. Unless there is some transgression of the rules relating to copyright, the library is able to request such materials. In the electronic world this is much less clear and will not become any more certain until Congress updates the various copyright statutes, while actions by other countries may have other kinds of impacts. The international nature of information is likely to have an increasing influence on library programs.

Further complications are the right of public access, and the right of the public to retrieve public information. Although these issues relate mostly to information that is in the public domain, the legal issues also cover what is protected by copyright and what is freely available as a public good. The rights of individuals are related closely to the needs and rights of libraries. Here, there are also problems relating to free speech, pornography, parental rights, and the role of the library in protecting free access to information. To date, judicial decisions have generally favored free access, but there are also suggestions that there may be problems between the competing rights of several groups. The whole issue of electronic privacy is under congressional investigation, and the resulting determinations may have profound effects on what libraries can and cannot do.

For the library, the budgetary implication is that it must be prepared to support public access to information, although such access need not always be without cost to the individual user. The library must always be careful to distinguish between public and individual goods, and to decide what it can and cannot do from its own funds.

Notes

1. The basic U.S. code is the "National Interlibrary Loan Code, 1993" (Chicago: Reference and Adult Services Division [RASD], 1994) reprinted from *RQ,* Fall 1994. Additional guidelines are "Guidelines and Procedures for Telefacsimile and Electronic Delivery of Interlibrary Loan Requests" (Chicago: RASD, 1994), also published in *RQ;* "Guidelines for Packaging and Shipping Microforms" (Chicago: Association for Library Collections and Technical Services, 1989); and "Guidelines for the Loan of Rare and Unique Materials" (Chicago: Association of College and Research Libraries, 1993), published in *College & Research Library News,* May 1993. These and many other similar standards and guidelines are listed in the large annual edition of the *ALA Handbook of Organization and Membership Directory.* States, consortia, and other groups of libraries have also developed codes, most of which are designed to address local conditions, particularly the needs of smaller libraries.

2. There have been numerous cost studies, dating from the early 1970s. Some were extremely elaborate, e.g., those by King Associates designed to assist in copyright law revisions; others are relatively simple, such as that by J. E. Herstand, "Interlibrary Loan Cost Study and Comparison" *RQ* 20 (1981): 249–56. Care should always be taken in interpreting such studies, since the conditions surrounding them can have changed substantially since the time of publication.

3. "Decision Rules for Access," chapter 7 in *The Economics of Access versus Ownership,* ed. Bruce R. Kingma (Binghamton, N.Y.: Haworth Press, 1996).

4. Jody Bates Foote and Roland C. Reson, "The Unexpected Effect of Online Databases on Undergraduate Use of Interlibrary Loan," *Journal of Interlibrary Loan, Document Delivery & Information Supply* 5, no. 4 (1995): 65–72.

5. Marilyn M. Roche, *ARL/RLG Interlibrary Loan Cost Study: A Joint Effort by the Association of Research Libraries and the Research Libraries Group* (Washington, D.C.: ARL, 1993).

6. F. K. Rottman, "To Buy or Borrow: Studies of the Impact of Interlibrary Loan on Collection Development in the Academic Library," *Journal of Interlibrary Loan & Document Supply* 1, no. 3 (1991): 17–27.

7. Representative articles are those by Tom Davenport, "Think Tank: Knowledge Roles; The CKO and Beyond," *CIO* (April 1, 1996): 24–26, and Stan Davis and Jim Botlin, "The Coming of Knowledge-Based Business," *Harvard Business Review* (September/October 1994): 165–70.

8. While there is not yet a comparable kind of approach in library literature, the following articles suggest that librarians have begun to understand the importance of librarianship in the age of information: Stephen B. Goddard, "The Information Superhighway: Crisis & Opportunity," *Library Journal* 119, ho. 12 (July 1994): 56; Arlene G. Taylor, "The Information Universe: Will We Have Chaos or Control?" *American Libraries* 25, no. 7 (July/August 1994): 629–32; Marilyn Gell Mason, "The Future Revisited," *Library Journal* 121, no. 12 (July 1996): 70–72, about the role of public libraries; Jorge Reina Schement, "A 21st-Century Strategy for Librarians," *Library Journal* 121, no. 8 (May 1, 1996): 34–36; Cynthia N. James-Catalano, "Library Links," *Internet World* 7, no. 7 (July 1996): 32–34.

9. Interloan in New Zealand is an agreement between participating libraries and is based on the idea that borrowing and lending by any one library should balance out. *Library Life* (the newsletter of the New Zealand Library and Information Association) publishes lists of net lending and net borrowing libraries along with suggestions of where to send requests.

10. Charges for lending are becoming more and more common. These may include both basic fees and charges for photocopy or other out-of-pocket expenditures.

11. Among such directories are Roxann Bustos, comp. *Interlibrary Loan in College Libraries* (Chicago: ACRL, 1993. Clip Note #16); Virginia Boucher, *Interlibrary Loan Practices Handbook,* 2nd ed. (Chicago: American Library Association, 1996); and Leslie R. Morris and Sandra C. Morris, *Interlibrary Loan Policies Directory,* 4th ed. (New York: Neal-Schuman, 1991). Readers should be aware that all such information dates quickly.

12. Among the nonlibrary publications on copyright, "Copyrights," by Eric R. Chapman, *Information Week,* no. 572 (March 25, 1996): 46–54, may be cited as presenting a full picture of the problems surrounding copyright in the present age, while the periodical *Internet* has a frequent column on legal issues which could be studied with great profit by librarians.

13. *Intellectual Property and the National Information Infrastructure: The Report of the Working Group on Intellectual Property Rights,* Bruce A. Lehman, Chair (Washington, D.C.: U.S. Department of Commerce, 1995). Some idea of the divisions between librarians and publishers can be gathered from the two-part presentation, "The Great Copyright Debate: Two Experts Face Off," by Carol A. Risher and Laura N. Gasaway, *Library Journal* 115 (September 15, 1994): 34–37.

14. Australia, Canada, and New Zealand are all working on revisions of their laws regarding copyright, mostly in reaction to the latest General Agreement on Trade and Tariffs (GATT), but also in an attempt to grapple with changes in the information world itself. These reviews are in various stages of completion and the U.S. Congress is also looking at possible copyright law revisions. Librarians in Canada have expressed some reservations about proposed changes, though it seems unlikely that there will be any action before this book is ready for publication. This note is meant to remind librarians that legal developments in other countries can be of importance to them. The recent problems with China over the pirating of CDs and videos underline the publishers' deep concerns over copyright and how these can influence national policy. Legal changes worldwide can greatly impact international interlibrary loan. Recent concerns over pornography on the Internet revealed how difficult it is to insert any national control mechanism into an international communications network and underlines the differences between printed and electronic publications.

8

Document Delivery

Because most libraries now find it increasingly difficult to provide all needed information on-site, they are turning to other forms of delivery. While the delivery of specific publications, whether reprinted or electronic, to the individual user may seem to be outside the scope of acquisitions, it merely represents the extension in a somewhat different way of the long-standing alternative to purchase, interlibrary loan. As will be shown below some of the surrounding circumstances are different, but they continue the drive by the library to provide each user with wanted materials, whether they are available locally or not. In this sense document delivery is a direct component of acquisitions, but what is acquired by this process is intended for the exclusive use of one customer, in the same way articles procured via interlibrary loan become the property of the library user. If a library is interested in maximum service to its users, all modes of supplying information have to be used.

The budgetary problems that have speeded up the shift toward information delivery rather than information purchase have been caused largely by rapid price increases for scientific and technical journals, as ably explored by Dennis Carrigan.[1] The long-standing national and worldwide interlibrary loan system has proved unable to cope with the resulting deluge of requests, largely because other budget problems precluded the addition of staff to meet the demand, and many libraries are looking increasingly to document delivery as the solution. The phrase suggests simply handing over needed information but is, in fact, far more complicated. It includes recovery and delivery services, fees for users, and reimbursement to information providers.

Many of the budget-related aspects of this library shift were well presented by Ardis and Croneis in their article on the relationships between document delivery, serials budgets, and cost containment almost ten years ago,[2] while Anna Perrault has reported extensively on the changes in the printed information resource base in academic libraries leading to a wider use of access.[3] From another perspective, document delivery can be seen as a reaching out to the world.[4] These conflicting views explain in part why libraries have had difficulty in reconciling these different strategies. The need to hold down permanent costs, as represented best by rising serial prices, has led to incurring many smaller, occasional costs, as represented by individual transactions, in the hope that these would total less in the long run. This aim appears to be confirmed by reports from the Louisiana State University, where document delivery requests for articles rather than requests for subscriptions may well have reduced direct costs by an order of 20–25 percent.[5] Further information from the same source indicates that actual user needs do not always coincide with their stated preferences for subscriptions. Nevertheless, even these favorable statistics do not tell the whole story. In order to make final decisions, librarians would need to know the whole range of costs involved, not simply savings from cancellations. Libraries need to minimize their costs, but cannot readily do so in a world where those costs are difficult to determine.

As distinct from interlibrary loan, document delivery is a personal transaction, usually in a business setting, somewhat like a fee-based service, and fee-based service units do carry a great deal of document delivery as part of their routine activities. Mostly, however, libraries using the term document delivery imply simply a user service for which there will be a charge. Cost recovery is thus an important consideration. There are other situations in which the library has decided that it can provide funds to support document retrieval, i.e., the George Washington University "Scholars' Express," but most libraries have to recover their costs when transactions fall outside their usual parameters. The budget transactions involved are by no means simple, if, for example, it proves necessary to add staff to meet new demands. Because document delivery is often a major element in fee-based services, librarians contemplating setting up such a service may well want to read Suzanne Ward's book on setting up fee-based services in academic libraries.[6]

Commercial Suppliers

A second consideration is that it will often be necessary to involve commercial suppliers because other libraries are unable to respond as directly. While these may sometimes be used in ILL, they are more likely to be directly involved in document delivery, partly because it reduces the number of participants, but also because they are used to dealing with such transactions. These relationships introduce quite new cost factors, since commercial suppliers must recover their costs and make a profit if they are to survive. This statement is not a pejorative one, since all businesses need to make some profit. In fact, libraries are becoming more and more sensitive to the need to pass on some of their costs if they are to survive.

Differences from Interlibrary Loan

Although, on the face of it, both are in the business of providing documents, there are several important differences between document delivery and interlibrary loan. ILL is a library-to-library transaction, controlled by a wide range of protocols, conventions, and legal considerations. What can and cannot be done depends on the interpretation of a wide range of statutory rules and regulations. By and large, for example, its proper use does not incur royalty payments—the British Library Document Delivery Service has, however, decided to impose royalties in keeping with its movement away from simply providing interlibrary loan—but may often involve charges for the costs of photocopying and transmitting the resulting information. Document delivery, however, as a regular business transaction, is subject to all the rules relating to copyright, royalty payments, and other publisher and supplier charges. These charges are passed on to the user.

Document delivery will seldom deal with complete "books" and similar publications. In this context, that is more properly the domain of a bookseller. It may, occasionally, handle such transactions using suppliers prepared to provide print copies of tape or microform publications, e.g., UMI of Ann Arbor in the case of dissertations. The cost is, however, likely to be a deterrent to most library users. The same may not be true in future for electronic publications, where a document delivery service might be much better able to handle downloading, including the problems likely to be associated with permissions and payments. For the foreseeable future, however, the lending and borrowing of printed books is likely to remain the domain of ILL.

Similarly, document delivery may face some limitations in handling international materials. While document delivery may well be the library agency that deals with the British Library Document Delivery Service, in many countries there is no such mechanism available. Some commercial services, such as UnCover, Inc., have developed international contacts and can supply a wide range of materials, albeit from a limited number of other countries. As with all such arrangements, librarians will have to look for alternative ways of providing materials that cannot be so supplied.[7] How these are meshed together will be determined by the mission and the resources of the library.

Electronic Access

The rapid emergence of electronic information networks suggests an added role for document delivery. The growing range of databanks, either on- or offline, makes it feasible for libraries to provide access to a wider range of materials than they could possibly purchase. Most large libraries, for example, either provide direct user access to databanks, or can provide access through various commercial services, sometimes alongside the library's own catalog. For the most part, this activity has been part of reference service, but it would seem reasonable to add at least the supply responsibility to document delivery. This would have the additional advantage of combining financial service points. Doing so may require some reconstruction in the library, since it would be awkward to have search centers and supply centers widely separated. Some of these issues are explored from a New Zealand perspective by Michael Wooliscroft.[8] Clearly there are great advantages to electronic transactions when the request's point of origin is far separated from most likely suppliers. This can also apply to an isolated library even in a country such as the United States which is also a resource-rich country. In this context, isolated need not imply only the wide spaces of the West, but such situations as the "Northeast Kingdom," in Vermont, where access to other collections is extremely difficult for both geographic and financial reasons.

The way in which any such service is set up will reflect the library's arrangements for online access, which will often reflect, in turn, a series of institutional decisions. Even its physical location can be determined by the nature of the local network, the need for sufficient space for a range of equipment, and the need for easy patron access.

Library Initiation

Although document delivery is mostly thought of as customer initiated, there are settings in which the library staff may suggest to the user that document delivery would best suit his or her purpose. For example, a long and complex search of a database may well result in the discovery of a wide range of documents the library does not own. Traditional ILL can handle some of this, but it may be that document delivery via a commercial supplier would be more expeditious. Moreover, a quasi-business operation is better equipped to deal with such things as credit cards, personal and departmental accounts, and any special delivery requirements. These variations suggest that libraries need to develop ways to cope more completely with the increasing complexity of the financial world.

Alternatives

There will also be times when the user does not want to follow the procedures laid down for ILL and would prefer to pay for a different service. This is often the case when it is possible to proceed directly from a database search to document recovery without having to shift to another part of the organization. This is quite different from user-originated ILL, which mostly has on-site vetting by the ILL staff built into the process to avoid sending out for materials owned by the library. Sometimes it is easier for an organizationally separate part of an institution, e.g., a research institute, to use document delivery and have the documents delivered directly to the person wanting them. In all these cases there has been some library or institutional staff intervention.

While there may seem little difference between the kinds of activities listed above and direct user-originated requests, they are set out here to show there are occasions where the library staff may make a deliberate choice in favor of document delivery and so direct the library patron.

Customer Initiation

The commonest kind of document delivery request is initiated by the customer, who has already assembled at least rudimentary information on what is wanted, and simply wants the materials supplied. This is most likely with corporate and business requests made of public libraries, such as through the San Francisco Public Library's Library Express program, but can often result from preliminary work carried out in the course of a research project. It may also be the preferred choice of a small firm or research corporation that does not want to accumulate its own library and does not have the staff resources to carry out library research. These kinds of needs tend to ally with fee-based library services and should certainly be separated out financially.[9] Tax-supported libraries need to look carefully at how document delivery is handled and financed in order to avoid conflicts of interest internally and tax issues externally.

Generally speaking, customer-initiated requests will require more preparatory staff work and this will increase the cost to the user, though many libraries are moving toward similar base charges for ILL. In setting up any such service, a library must be prepared either to cover its entire costs in tracking information or to advise would-be users that they must complete their own initial checking of bibliographic information before asking for a specific document. On the other hand, such services as those provided by the National Technical Information Service (NTIS), which use numbering systems for document identification, may well be best handled through document delivery. It is always, however, necessary to consider the issue of whether the benefits are directly personal or contain some element of institutional service.

Budgetary Effects

To the degree that document delivery is seen as a self-supporting activity, it can be thought of as off-budget. This does not mean that it does not have to work out a budgetary strategy and maintain financial records, only that these will be separate from the rest of the library budget records, even if they are only set up as a self-contained account. Care must be taken not to allow other library support to spill over into the account, *unless* it is being run as a subsidized service.[10] This is the setting of the Scholars' Express at George Washington University, where funds from cancelled serial subscriptions were set aside to pay for the recovery of documents needed by faculty and students. There may be limitations, e.g., only so many searches per semester or on the number of free pages, and service may be limited to faculty and graduate students.

In this way document delivery is still a free or subsidized library service, even though it is financially separate. Librarians who see subsidized document delivery as a way of making up for serial cancellations should pay close attention to the available records of what is actually needed and wanted. These may not always correspond with cancellations. Indeed, some records have suggested that there was little need for the subscription in the first place.[11] This does not in any way reduce the importance of such cancellation programs; it merely underlines the fact that libraries need to learn much more about their users, their needs, and their patterns of activity.

Nevertheless there will still be some overall effect on library budget planning, particularly if document delivery is seen as a way of reducing the number of interlibrary loan transactions or as a kind of extension of existing photocopy services. As Anne Woodsworth suggested directly about electronic services, cost allocation has become even more pressing as a planning issue than cost recovery.[12] Estimating future growth and, therefore, future budget proportions is extremely difficult without an extensive history to fall back on. Calling on past history can be relevant, as, for example, the rapid expansion of interlibrary loan with the improvement of OCLC and similar systems. All libraries will need to look closely at use patterns. Too few libraries have sought extensive information on the kinds of uses made of their collections and services. Without such information, librarians must be searching in the dark when they try to determine what kinds of resources and services they will need.

User Patterns As Budget Guides

Systematic, in-depth study of user patterns has not been characteristic of library planning in the past, but will undoubtedly be a part of all such planning in the future, as it is of the groundbreaking cost benefit study conducted by Coopers & Lybrand for New Zealand libraries,[13] or some of the work carried out by Paul Kantor at Case Western Reserve University.[14] Librarians must consider closely what strategies are most likely to match their service goals and what kinds of charges or trade-offs are most appropriate.[15] Whereas academic libraries may seek to generate a budget reserve from serial cancellations and then to charge access fees to this reserve, few public libraries can exercise such an option. The major example is the Scholars' Express service funded by George Washington University with funds generated by serial cancellations, since emulated by several other universities. Here the costs of document recovery for articles from serials no longer held by the university are paid for from funds set aside from having cancelled serials subscriptions. Clearly such funds can be used only for the local community, and it would be important to differentiate between local and external users. This is a salutory reminder to keep internal and external services and costs separated. If document delivery is run as part of a fee-based service unit, some of these problems will not arise.

Document delivery thus is likely to operate within a much more clearly delineated sphere of user benefit, and libraries will have to adjust their operations to recognize this fact. Borrowing owned materials differs greatly from seeking non-owned materials. When there are also two different communities involved, local and other, it becomes necessary to differentiate the resulting transactions. It may even be necessary to maintain two sets of accounts, if there are local subsidies to be provided, in order to differentiate between local and distant users.

Summary

Although most of these issues will be discussed in more detail in later chapters, all librarians undertaking or proposing document delivery services should be aware that they are changing significantly their way of doing business. Whereas it was relatively simple to deal with publishers and other libraries when it was simply a matter of purchasing a specific item, there are significant differences in the online information world, not least of them questions concerning copyright. There are also cost differences, though these may be reduced as the world of electronic information retrieval expands, since it will no longer be a matter of simply reproducing an existing artifact but of producing a clone. The rights of the author, the publisher, the user, and the library may be in conflict. Although it is possible to harmonize these rights, the process can be extremely complex. In this situation, it may well be easiest to handle these problems in a separate business unit. Any library which proposes to set up some kind of document delivery service should look carefully at the effects on its not-for-profit status and plan accordingly.

This may seem a nonconclusion, but it is the best resolution that can be achieved in the present copyright setting. Librarians must continue to look at legal and judicial decisions regarding copyright and similar legal settings. The ways in which it is appropriate to serve members and nonmembers can differ greatly. Unless this difference is observed a library can find itself in great trouble.

Notes

1. Dennis P. Carrigan, "Commercial Journal Publishers and University Libraries: Retrospect and Prospect," *Journal of Scholarly Publishing* 27, no. 4 (July 1996): 208–21.

2. Susan B. Ardis and Karen B. Croneis, "Document Delivery, Cost Containment, and Serials Ownership," *College & Research Library News* 48 (November 1987): 624–27.

3. Anna H. Perrault, "The Changing Print Resource Base of Academic Libraries in the United States," *Journal of Education for Library and Information Science* 36, no. 4 (Fall 1995): 295–308.

4. Mounir Khalil, "Reaching the World through Document Delivery," in *Proceedings of the 14th National Online Meeting* (New York: 1993), 233–40.

5. Jane P. Kleiner and Charles A. Hamaker, "Libraries 2000: Transforming Libraries Using Document Delivery, Needs Assessment, and Networked Resources," *College & Research Libraries* 58, no. 4 (July 1997): 355–74.

6. Suzanne M. Ward, *Starting and Managing Fee-Based Information Services in Academic Libraries* (Greenwich, Conn.: JAI Press, 1997).

7. Wayne Pederson and David Gregory, "Interlibrary Loan and Commercial Document Supply: Finding the Right Fit," *Journal of Academic Librarianship* 20, no. 5/6 (November 1994): 263–72; Mary E. Jackson, "Integrating ILL with Document Delivery: Five Models," *Wilson Library Bulletin* (September 1993): 76–78.

8. Michael Wooliscroft, "Access and Ownership: Academic Libraries, Collecting and Service Responsibilities, and the Emerging Benefits of Electronic Publishing and Document Supply," *New Zealand Libraries* 47, no. 5 (March 1994): 170–80.

9. *Fiscal Facts,* the publication of Fee-Based Information Service Centers in Academic Libraries, a discussion group of the Association of College and Research Libraries, contains useful pointers and discussions.

10. For a brief survey of the alternatives see William L. Whitson, "The Way I See It: Free, Fee, or Subsidy? The Future Role of Libraries," *College & Research Library News* 55, no. 7 (July–August 1994): 426–27.

11. Lynne C. Branche, "Document Delivery: Where Collection Development and ILL Meet: An RASD Collection Development and Evaluation Section Program," *Library Acquisitions: Practice and Theory* 18 (1994): 96–97.

12. Anne Woodsworth and J. F. Williams II, *Managing the Economics of Owning, Leasing, and Contracting Out Information Services* (Brookfield, Vt.: Ashgate, 1993), 139.

13. Coopers & Lybrand, *Valuing the Economic Costs and Benefits of Libraries. A Study Prepared for the N Strategy* (Wellington: New Zealand Library and Information Association, 1996).

14. Paul Kantor, *Levels of Output Related to Cost of Operation of Scientific and Technical Libraries: The Final Report of the LORCOST Libraries Project* (Cleveland, Ohio: Department of Systems Engineering, Case Western Reserve University) n.d.

15. As David Taylor suggested many years ago, charges for electronic access may be as inevitable as charges for photocopy, since the alternative is to bankrupt the budget. His study, "Serials Management: Issues and Recommendations," in *Issues in Library Management: A Reader for the Professional Librarian* (White Plains, N.Y.: Knowledge Industry Publishers, 1984), 82–96, is still relevant.

9

Electronic Alternatives

The creation and the extension of the Internet, or its various metamorphoses, such as the World Wide Web, have spawned an entire new world of information creators and suppliers. While the Internet itself is a cranky, chaotic construct, many of its users are carefully constructing specific niches, while both profit and nonprofit enterprises are acting to ensure both their presence and their survival, notable among which are the many personal, municipal, and institutional home pages. The implications for libraries are both tantalizing and threatening. On the one hand, the Internet holds out the hope of access to hitherto inaccessible information. On the other hand, the commercial and legal issues promise to become a quagmire in which the best of intentions may be submerged.[1] The balancing act required will mean that librarians, publishers, and software/hardware vendors must work much more closely together than has been possible in the past. As distinct from the world of print, where each artifact had a clear physical existence, in the "cyberworld" such notions as existence are at best tenuous. Similarly, the equivalents of reading, browsing, or skimming are not yet readily definable, while downloading has no exact equivalent in the print world, other than photocopy which is much less precise in terms of copying and publishing. There are also problems with the maintenance of "textual" integrity. The mere use of these undefinable terms indicates how far we are from developing appropriate terminology for the electronic age. Unless providers and users can find more common ground, the unlimited promise of the new medium may diminish or vanish.

Unless such a convergence of purposes takes place the ordinary user (i.e., in older terms, the reader) may well be shortchanged. Some of these concerns were well expressed by Kaplan and Rogers in "The Silicon Classroom," where they pointed out that neither the producers nor the teachers knew the best ways of using computers. Indeed, there are many stories circulating about young students who are better able to handle computers than are their teachers. There are added cautions. "Computer literacy doesn't necessarily generate the traditional kind. Indeed the Internet may breed a new kind of intellectual laziness." Their emphasis on the need for added training is also a warning for librarians, and, a note to wouldbe purchasers, "neither the physical nor the administrative structure exists to help the poor purchasing agents."[2] These points are placed in a library setting by Young and Peters, who remind librarians that technology comes neither easily nor cheaply.[3] These points should be kept in mind when looking at the current programs for linking every school and library to the Internet.

To date, at least in the United States, access to the Internet has not carried a specific fee, unless a commercial service was being used. Even these are adopting many marketing strategies, including flat fees and an allowance of free time but, as the number of suppliers dwindles, there may be significant increases in access costs. Moreover, the U.S. government has made it clear that it wants commercial interests to help expand the electronic network. Libraries should be pleased that they have been able to achieve a special status, with reduced charges, but they should not become complaisant. Indeed, that status has already been challenged. There are, also, the costs associated with setting up access stations, the maintenance of hardware and software (the need for increasing bandwidth renders most hardware and software obsolete very rapidly), and the various telecommunications protocols associated with worldwide communication. These kinds of problems make the role of the library extremely difficult, mostly because few, if any, libraries, whether academic, public, or school, are in a position to make independent budgetary decisions in this kind of setting. Even when the parent institution is supportive, it may seek to implement programs that are not necessarily in the library's best interest, for example by using internal programs not suited to worldwide communication or getting cheap but incompatible equipment.

The Library and the Internet

In the comfortable chaos that has so far prevailed, none of the access costs have been directed at the library or the individual user. This setting may well change abruptly as the various international agreements and protocols on copyright and information sharing are established. This level of international activity affirms that information has finally become an economic good and thus subject to all the laws, rules, and regulations that affect most commercial products. Clearly, products without a physical existence defy most existing rules and regulations but will eventually become subject to a new set of international agreements and laws. This process is under way but the cumbersome nature of international negotiations followed by multiple legislation by many countries may well make any decisions await the next millennium. For the present libraries will continue to operate in a kind of legal vacuum. Slowly this situation will be improved, but librarians need to remain deeply involved in all the negotiations surrounding access to electronic information. Unless they do, it is quite possible that they will find themselves excluded from the electronic community.

Changes in the Library Community

From a library perspective, the most troubling issue is that electronic access imports a whole new world of resources and users. Instead of a world where distance and time zones clearly defined who could use a specific library, the virtual collapse of both makes it possible for the whole world to become part of the library's clientele.

- Who is a part of the library community?
- Does it include anyone who has access, no matter how remote?
- Are the rules the same for all participants?
- What resources are accessible? Is there a charge?
- If so, how will it be levied and paid?

These questions may seem readily resolvable—simply expunge requests from nonlocal users. But, what if those users are distant students, corporate clients, or participants in a research endeavor? In such situations the library still has a research support role, but now one which may include a wide range of formerly cash-only activities. Moreover, there will remain the question of what kinds of help should be extended to distant libraries where there may be some kind of shared activity. Few major research projects are conducted nowadays solely on one campus and some may even extend into space. Similarly, companies and research establishments are seldom confined to one physical location or one country. In most cases the supporting organization will provide some kind of electronic network support—with the presumption that its use will not involve further costs. A good example is the headquarters of the Merrill Lynch complex in New York, which is more "wired" than many small countries. Libraries will need to negotiate carefully their use of "cyberspace." Not only do they have to determine what kinds of access they will provide; they have to determine whether they will charge for that access, and what kinds of charges they will levy for which users.

- Who can use the library?
- What can they use?
- Will there be a charge for certain uses?
- Are these universal charges?
- Will there be a charge for personal online accounts?
- Are there reciprocal agreements with other libraries?

These questions simply touch the surface of an increasingly complex situation, but answering them is essential if the library is to develop a true resource budget.

Changes in the Supply of Information

The range of information resources available has changed dramatically, to include hard data, online databases, a wide range of electronic publications that may have an equally wide range of user controls, for example encryption, and that may be subject to user charges, and the equivalent of endless personal correspondence. Though the latter may not figure widely in a library administration's perception of electronic information, this view may not be shared by some of the library's users, such as those who need to consult personal records when exploring the history of a publication or the life of an individual.[4] This kind of expansion simply adds to the library's problems, not the least of them being public concern about access to undesirable materials. Although the American Library Association has not yet taken an official position on the use of access control mechanisms, called filters, they have already been installed in many libraries. The decision by the Supreme Court that the legislation in question was contrary to the Fifth Amendment's guarantee of free speech still leaves libraries, particularly public libraries, having to deal with parental and special-interest challenges to the right of free access to the Internet. There are so many intellectual freedom issues involved that it is almost impossible to suggest a single solution. Librarians should, however, be careful not to restrict their users beyond what is legally necessary.

Organizational Issues

Few, if any, libraries have the resources to provide all electronic access by themselves. In all likelihood, the major technical support will be provided by the computer center in a university, and it may be a town- or citywide activity in the case of public libraries. A further possibility is for a group of libraries to work together in order to lower the cost to the individual library. This is the equivalent of resource sharing in the world of print. These arrangements can be problematic for libraries. For example, we can recall having to explain at length why the library wanted to maintain open access at all its OPAC terminals all the time. The computer center staff found it difficult to believe that we could not control who used what terminal when! Similar differences of viewpoint can be expected to emerge as new issues are faced. Not least of them will be concerns with territoriality, all of which can be expected to have some kind of budgetary component. How and by whom these new costs should be paid within an institution may become a vexing question. Even a public library, accustomed to going it alone, may find that there are many unanswered questions, as was discovered by the San Franciso Public Library after the expansion of its central facility and the subsequent growth of services.

Costs   In any event, the library has now brought into its orbit a whole new range of costs, not least of which is the need to provide a sinking fund to cover the replacement of outdated hardware and software.[5] Few, if any institutions have provided such funds in the past, relying rather on special tax levies, loans, or fund-raising when the needs arise. These methods no longer suffice in a time when the life of the equipment in question may well be rather less than five years. The responsibility for setting up such a fund must be determined, and many libraries do not have the authority to set aside replacement funds on their own initiative. The purchase of capital equipment may also be subject to much stricter controls than other kinds of payments and may require a different set of approvals. Sometimes, when the amount of financing required is substantial, a city may require a bond levy, while a university may decide to borrow the necessary funds. Negotiating this kind of purchase can be tortuous indeed.

Who Provides the Service?

Because it is often a shared service, for example with computer services or the local government, it is necessary to decide who is responsible for repairs and general maintenance and who will pay those costs.

- Where will the support staff be housed and what budget will pay for them?
- Are these costs going to be prorated and how will the library's share be determined?
- If an outside party is used to provide the service, who pays for what, and what procedure must be followed?
- Who decides when and if upgrades will be implemented?
- Who will represent the library on any advisory or control committee?
- How will any bids for replacement or renewal of any contract be handled?

Although these may seem procedural or governmental issues, the answers will often decide what charges will be levied on the library and how those charges will be determined. There can be a great deal of difference between charges that have been negotiated in a friendly setting and those imposed by fiat or by an external agency without library input.

Libraries must be vigilant in order to determine how best to serve their constituents. Only too often other agencies will readily take over a relinquished responsibility. Because more and more of the library's budget is likely to be spent on charges for services, the library has to be wary lest it be exploited, even by its own service agencies. These issues are addressed by Evan St. Lifer, in a *Library Journal* article on Internet costs.[6] Although there is no apparent need, now, to be wary of the kinds of charges levied by Internet providers, the problems experienced by America Online suggest that libraries should be very careful when negotiating a service contract. They may, of course, be included in contracts made by their controlling authorities and thus have no option. They may also have rules about setting up personal accounts whereby the individual becomes directly responsible for any costs involved. This may, however, be somewhat similar to the use of online databases, where the library becomes the agent and will therefore have to bear the cost of collecting any payments due to the provider, and reminds us of the increasingly uncertain financial relationship between library and user.

Shifting Emphases

The electronic access network which is likely to provide a major proportion of the future library's services is more complex than simply plugging into a telephone service, though that, too, is becoming much more complex. It involves a much wider range of indirect services and may also result in a new set of direct charges to users, especially if the library has arranged to provide electronic access for individuals through individual accounts. Libraries need to consider the effects of such agreements and the ways in which the resulting charges will be paid, whether by the library (i.e., the community) or by the individual.

There are clearly some activities that are equivalent to the use of books or other printed materials, but there are others that more closely resemble photocopying, for example downloading. Any of these activities may also be affected by actions on the part of the provider in establishing use charges. There is even the possibility that an online publisher may charge simply for browsing. The library needs to sort through these differences and commonalities in setting its policies.

The Relationship between the Individual and the Library

While it is clear that electronic access widens the ability of the individual to access information, it is not yet clear whether the associated costs are such as can be absorbed by libraries or whether they need to to be passed on to the individual user. In the latter setting, there is also the need to decide whether only the direct or all associated costs will be charged. In the increasingly commercial setting of online information, charging only direct costs may lead to problems with the IRS, since the library is conducting a business and failure to charge back indirect costs may create a problem. Although this may seem a kind of doomsayer approach, librarians must be wary of finding themselves caught in the setting of conducting a commercial enterprise without adequate prior preparation.

Shared Services

Because of their cost, electronic services have often been separated from general library services. This may beg the question of equal access but recognizes that libraries cannot supply unlimited electronic services to their users without serious economic consequences. As a response, many libraries have sought to combine their resources in order to establish a more satisfactory economic basis for such services.[7] The same arguments can be applied to all library transactions. Nothing is costless and determining who pays can be a complex and unrewarding task. In part, it is a matter of what falls within the library's mandate; in part, a matter of competition between private and public goods. No one is likely to suggest that this will be an easy problem to solve, but, equally, no one should presume to have the answers at hand, or that there is no answer.

Electronic information services are based on the presumption that users will want to pay for the answers they receive. This is a legitimate business perception but may not always apply to the library situation, where much information is free, in the sense that no additional costs accrue to the user. Libraries must, therefore, look at the ways they will adapt their traditional services to encompass electronic services. Books were bought and therefore owned and there were no further author or publisher interests in how they were used (except in countries with author rights), but electronic publications may well have different sets of guidelines. Sales of books generate royalties to their authors and profits to their publishers, but electronic publications may not do so unless there are the same applications of copyright and similar legal definitions.

- Do the same kinds of understandings apply in the electronic world?
- If so, how do libraries cope with such charges?
- Should all users be assessed for their use of texts online, or should the library absorb all or some of these costs as part of its service contract?
- Can the library subsidize certain kinds of uses, while charging for others?

Unless these questions are addressed and answered, libraries and their governing institutions will continue to have problems in the electronic information age. The basic problem is the relationship between the creator, the publisher, and the user of information. Libraries, as the holders of published information, are caught uneasily in the middle. They have no direct right of ownership in electronic materials, except the tenuous one set out in any lease or similar contract, but they also have a duty to provide their users with the information that is available. How these rights and duties should be reconciled will become clear only with the passage of time.

Contractual Relationships

Many of the relationships between libraries and information providers will move from direct sale to contractual relationships. Whereas a sale transferred a book or other product from the ownership of the provider to that of the purchaser, it is not always as clear whether the adoption of an access contract clearly transfers ownership or even full access rights to the library. Most such transactions are governed by another kind of legal definition—contract law. The library may or may not have the right to reuse such materials without having to pay for that use. This may seem a purely legal question, but librarians need to be reminded that legal questions now control much of their activity. The rights of the library may be defined by the original contract, but may also involve rights within a consortial agreement. These situations may be revisited if Congress picks up again the matter of electronic copyright, as it must almost certainly do in the light of the various international conferences and agreements that have taken place recently.

Memberships

Membership in a consortium or dealer group might seem to resolve or at least simplify many of the problems already cited, but it does not provide a panacaea against fraudulent or improper use of databases and similar information resources. To begin with, membership must include the right to access shared databases and provide for individual library access. Libraries wanting to enter into shared access programs need to look carefully at the defining characteristics. It may well be advantageous to share access to a range of online databases because any one library could not afford individual access, but it is well worth examining whether the agreement commits the library to long-term costs it cannot afford. The costs of these commitments are not solely in terms of library materials, but include personnel and operating costs. The last of these categories is becoming much more important in the electronic age.

In what may well be seen as a defining step by libraries, OhioLINK negotiated with Elsevier Electronic Subscriptions (EES) a three-year agreement providing the forty participating university and college libraries with full electronic access to the full text of the 1150 Elsevier Science journals. As was pointed out by Bill Studer, director of libraries at the Ohio State University, "no academic library in the state can begin to afford all these titles." The total cost for the three years is $23 million, approximately the cost of the current subscriptions. The difference, which may be crucial for many participants, is that all members have access to all the journals, whereas some of them could only afford thirteen paper subscriptions, and no single library subscribed to all the titles. There may still be questions about the costs of access and downloading, but the project illustrates the great differences between going it alone and acting within a consortium in the electronic age. This second deal follows on a earlier one with Academic Press, a three-year million dollar contract for 175 titles. More than thirty-five institutions worldwide have adopted EES.[8] While these actions may well presage the future, they leave uncertain the situation of a library which does not have such consortial support. In another sense they call into question the whole existence on paper of such journals of record, which could well have been functioning as a database for some time.

Cost Structures

There are two cost structures to consider. The first is that of the publisher. The cost of going electronic can be substantial[9] and may determine whether the publisher can follow this course. These considerations have to be accompanied by library considerations as to whether the options are equal.[10] The intermeshing of these two structures will have profound effects on library budgets in the future.

Traditional Budget Structures and Change

The structure of library budgets in the past has been based on three factors: staff, materials, and other support costs. While these factors will remain predominant, the character of the latter two ingredients is likely to change substantially. Library materials may well expand to include products that the library does not own, such as databases, and the "other" category will expand to include electronic access and its associated costs. To some extent these categories will overlap—it is less than clear who owns electronic information—and it will always be necessary to look at how the traditional library categories are involved in future library transactions. Moreover, it may be extremely difficult to extract the charges relating to any one transaction from the mass of accounting data accumulated. To some degree, this complexity explains the reluctance of librarians to undertake too great a level of cost recovery. The simple costs of billing patrons are often greater than the amount recovered.

Although libraries have not generally sought to set up individual user accounts, this may well be necessary when it is a matter of using electronic services. While it is often a matter of handling a specific request for information, which can then be charged back to the user, as is the case in the use of databases, electronic access may not be so easily defined. It may be necessary to establish a base name; it may also be necessary to set up a specific account; and it may be necessary to determine who will be responsible for any charges incurred. Librarians can decide to charge individual users for setting up an account and then charge them for any costs incurred. But this procedure is not likely to handle easily student and faculty charges that may have been incurred legitimately in their scholarly activity, including the pursuit of scholarly research. In such cases it may be necessary to determine whether these costs are legitimate research expenditures, whether some of the information could have been obtained locally, and whether there is any relationship to research grants and similar financial support.

Background Costs

The use of electronic information involves a range of costs far beyond those associated with printed information. Whereas printed materials involve specific processing and shelving costs, but are thereafter subject only to minimal transactional costs, such as circulation and reshelving (though the costs of housing printed materials are not to be discounted), electronic materials require that the library provide and support major electronic hardware and software. To date there has been very little study of such costs, to a large extent because it is very difficult to assign the costs of electronic access to either a specific publication or a specific publisher. Despite this difficulty, it is clear that the electronic library must look closely at the ancillary costs involved, because they tend to relate directly to the user rather than the library. The whole area of institutional responsibilities is likely to undergo major reexamination, and librarians must be aware of what is happening. It seems likely that librarians will have to look very closely at the ways in which they handle electronic transactions, and also at how they determine what can be provided free and what must be charged to the user.

Summary

The electronic age has changed some of the parameters of library/publisher relations but has not eliminated the need to be sure that the proposed use of the information in question is legitimate. Librarians need to be sure that they are aware of any charges levied by publishers or other agencies, and need to be aware of the kinds of demands being made by their users. Librarians continue to need to be able to assess the importance and the urgency of user needs before using the many electronic aids available. While this may seem heresy to those who regard the electronic universe as the only viable way to communicate, the fact remains that many, if not most, problems can most easily be solved by using traditional methods of investigation, including the use of printed reference materials.[11] The division of the library resource and service budget is now much more tricky than when it was only a question of the printed word. The gradual need to look at the reference function as part of the information access function has changed the organizational style of library budgets. The older rationales for resource expenditure no longer seem appropriate. It has been suggested that such old rules of thumb as 60:40, books:periodicals, are now defunct and that in the future it is now much more likely to be 40:30:30, books:periodicals:access.[12] The implication is a massive shift in the ways libraries purchase materials and equally massive changes in the way they provide services. If, as Paul Kobulnicky suggested in an interview, the age of serial-based information is over,[13] all libraries must think through again their budgeting process in order to determine where to put their money. The older allocations between personnel, materials, and support expenditures are no longer entirely adequate. All three kinds of expenditures are present in each and every library program. Some kind of program or transactional budget is the only way the effectiveness of library operations can be determined.

Notes

1. *Intellectual Property and the National Information Infrastructure: The Report of the Working Group on Intellectual Property Rights,* Bruce A. Lehmann, Chair (Washington, D.C.: U.S. Department of Commerce, 1995).

2. David A. Kaplan and Adam Rogers, "The Silicon Classroom," *Newsweek* 127, (April 22, 1996): 60–61. Both citations are from p. 61.

3. Arthur P. Young and Thomas A. Peters, "Reinventing Alexandria: Managing Change in the Electronic Library," *Journal of Library Administration* 22, no. 2/3 (1996): 21–41.

4. This is the subject of one review by Stephen Jay Gould in his book *An Urchin in the Storm: Essays about Books and Ideas* (New York: Norton, 1987), where he

suggests that the loss of personal written records may be a serious problem for the historians of science. Libraries concerned with the history of science should pay close attention to this issue.

5. John A. Dunn Jr. and Murray S. Martin, "The Whole Cost of Libraries," *Library Trends* 42, no. 3 (Winter 1993): 564–78.

6. Evan St. Lifer, "Public Libraries Budgets Brace for Internet Costs," *Library Journal* 122, no. 1 (January 1997): 44–47.

7. For the most part electronic sharing consists of forming consortia for the purchase of electronic databases or other products, but it may also be the result of working together to develop digitized resources. Some of these issues are well covered in an essay by Richard J. Cox, "Taking Sides on the Future of the Book," (*Library Journal* 122, no. 2 (February 1997): 153–55), part of a symposium on the future possibilities of print and electronic media.

8. "OhioLINK Cuts $23 Million Deal with Elsevier for Journals," *Library Journal* 122, no. 11 (June 15, 1997): 12.

9. Jack Meadows, David Pullinger, and Peter Such, "The Cost of Implementing an Electronic Journal," *Journal of Scholarly Publishing* 26, no. 4 (July 1995): 167–73; and Tom Clark, "On the Cost Differences between Publishing a Book in Paper and in the Electronic Medium," *Library Resources & Technical Services* 39, no. 1 (January 1995): 23–28.

10. Judy Luther, "Full Text Journal Subscriptions: An Evolutionary Process," *Against the Grain* 9, no. 3 (June 1997): 18, 20, 22, 24.

11. Walter Cronkite in an interview on WBUR (Boston), following the publication of his book *A Reporter's Life* (New York: Knopf, 1996), repeatedly stated that the only way to obtain adequate background information on any major topic is by reading printed resources. He did not downplay the role of electronic information, only pointed out that it is not suitable for extensive and prolonged consultation, but rather vectors in on readily presentable sound bites. Devoted cyberspace fans may dispute this, but it is worth asking whether any of them would be willing to "read" an entire electronic version of *War and Peace*.

12. Connie McCarthy in a personal communication to one of the authors, though the general idea is now widely present in both the printed and the electronic literature. Libraries have repeatedly sought ways to increase their "materials budget," often at the expense of services, but seem now to have come to perceive that the line between materials and services is, at best, difficult to draw. In the electronic age this distinction is becoming ever more blurred.

13. Murray S. Martin and Paul Kobulnicky, "The Role of the Library in Institutional Fundraising," *Bottom Line* 9, no. 1 (1996): 40–42. The general idea is supported by numerous reports about serial cancellations, which often suggest that the originals were not heavily used, and about the alternatives such as networks of scholars.

10

Budget Scenarios

The first requirement in developing a resource budget is to define the programs involved. The traditional library programs are set out below. To these would have to be added concerns with electronic media, document delivery, and interlibrary loan. Nevertheless this listing provides a framework for deciding what kinds of materials should be purchased and how. The general emphasis here was on the ways in which the library could acquire materials, but the same is true about any alternative budget system, whether the materials are acquired or accessed. The major difference is that a resource budget must expand its concerns with support expenditures, since these may vary greatly according to the method of information acquisition chosen.

Library Materials Programs

Direct purchase
    Publisher
    Dealer
    Agent

Approval plans and blanket orders

Subscriptions
    Direct
    Vendor

Standing orders
    Publisher
    Vendor

Gift and exchange
    Books
    Periodicals

Binding and mending

Other preservation measures

Purchase on demand

Leasing and renting

Replacement

Multiple copies

While this relatively simple budget may seem a truism left over from the days when program budgeting was most popular, it remains a basic tool for determining the institution's financial needs regardless of the manner in which the budget is finally constructed. In the context of this book, the most important factor is the changing nature of the programs within the library. It is now, for example, much less a matter of defining the acquisitions program (whether as a whole, as a separate object, or in program-related pieces) than of determining its relationship to other programs, such as interlibrary loan, document delivery, or online services. This is because making choices between different modes of access and delivery and determining their proportions of the whole change the budget of the entire library significantly.

The institutional environment is changing so rapidly that any advice can easily be outdated before it reaches print, but there are some general conditions that will continue to apply to all budgets.

- First, the supporting institution has to be able to set its budget needs in line with political realities.

- Second, the many financial strategies that have emerged recently, such as Responsibility Centered Management, have not yet been able fully to comprehend the needs of library and information services.[1]

- Third, libraries have to face the reality that many users prefer and are able to interact directly with information providers. The results may or may not be fully satisfactory, but most users have no way of determining whether that is so or not.

The library world has become so complex that it is somewhat foolhardy to attempt to set out an ideal budget, but the remaining chapters of this book will be concerned with the ways in which a resource budget can be established, without actually suggesting that any budget so presented is the answer to any individual library's concerns. The definition of any specific program is problematic, since individual library goals and needs differ so widely. Here the emphasis will be on using program definition as a way of determining the best choices a library can make in deciding how to deliver information, rather than in the more traditional sense of, say, acquisitions, reference services, children's services, or circulation services, all of which may well be involved in any specific information delivery mode. Even children's reading programs involve materials, staff, support services, and, frequently, donations of either time, materials, or money. When this process is extended to include electronic access, which may well be achievable from home or office, it is clear that the library has moved into an entirely different financial setting. It may well provide access to information, but the users may no longer need to visit the library, even if it is not a question of providing business information to distant users, the most common setting at present, but simply of helping users to log on to the Net, or ask for books to be reserved for their use, or to pick up messages on their library home page.

Program Definition

Because we are talking here principally about the delivery of information, the older division into Technical Processes and Public Services and their subsets becomes less meaningful. This does not mean that there are no future reference needs, nor that processing will vanish, only that the various activities may well have to be brought together in totally new ways in order to decide what mix of resources will best meet the goals of the library and the needs of its users. (Some of these relationships were set out in figure 5.1.) Each program will include personnel costs, materials costs, processing costs, service costs, *and* overhead costs. The latter are often overlooked when creating budgets, but must, in some way, be worked into the costs of the services provided by the library, as shown in figure 5.2. They will include not only administrative costs, but the costs associated with electronic services and the like, which call for expenditure on terminals, software, and time online. The infrastructure supporting technological access continues to climb in cost, most of which may be hidden in nonlibrary budgets, and, like the cost of accessing the Internet, may appear in the future as very unpleasant facts when it becomes necessary to budget for them directly. These kinds of indirect costs have always been present, but have usually been handled as part of an institutionwide overhead. Clearly, as such access becomes more widespread, any institution must look carefully at the costs involved and whether these are institutional or personal costs. Here, there is a significant social consideration, namely whether passing on the full costs may disenfranchise poorer users. This is the setting within which each library must determine whether it is willing (or able) to provide subsidies to some users.

Program Definitions

The first need is to define the programs provided by the library. The traditional terms, such as reference and lending, may not suffice, so librarians will have to look at what they are doing to derive appropriate program definitions.

- Who will benefit from the program?
- What kinds of benefits are derived?

- What are the associated costs?
- Can they be recouped from library users?
- Is there a way to determine user charges?
- If not, where should these costs be assigned in the library budget?

This analysis has seldom been carried out in the library world, or, indeed, in the business world. If it had, there might not have been as much concern with the San Francisco Public Library budget, which simply exposed what had become commonplace but not explicit within library budgets, for example the increasing cost of electronic support and the relationship between staffing and use levels.[2]

Program/Budget Relationships

Libraries must determine what programs they provide and develop budgets that reflect these decisions. If they do not, they will find it difficult to support their budget requests. The implication is that libraries must redefine their activities in terms that their supporting communities can understand. It is not sufficient to use such terms as reference, circulation, and technical processing to define the budget; the results of these classifications must be identified. Most library budgets in the past have been based on input factors, such as the number of books purchased. Future library budgets will have to be based on output factors, such as the number of requests fulfilled. Some of these issues are addressed by Nancy Van House and her coauthors in their book on measuring academic library performance. Another approach is shown in the study prepared for the New Zealand Library and Information Association by Coopers & Lybrand.[3] This may seem simple to do since it only means counting activities rather than counting books, but is truly a revolutionary way of perceiving the library budget. Allowing for the cautions suggested by John Budd,[4] we suggest that libraries now need to think much more clearly about services in their relation to people. It is not always easy to discover what people actually want, since only too often they will say they want what they think people expect them to want.[5] Budget constraints can force a conversation, but the results may not always be entirely useful. Robert Lent and his coauthors discuss this problem and suggest some answers.[6] Public libraries have had some success with citizen focus groups, as described by Linda Mielke.[7] Sometimes the results are not quite what you expected, but it is better to know more about the user community and its needs than to proceed according to some preconceived plan. The need, then, is to develop a series of factors that can be used to evaluate library programs in terms of services rendered.

How to Develop Factors

It may be difficult to evaluate reference transactions as such, but it will still be possible to look at such factors as information transferred, i.e., the equivalent of a loan. This assessment can also cover interlibrary loan transactions and similar library/user activities. Sometimes budget setters overlook such ordinary activities as in-house use of library materials, which may, especially in a college setting, greatly outnumber actual borrowings, and may also lead to other indicators, such as the number of photocopies made. Librarians do not always count the number of in-house uses, especially of periodical issues, even though these uses may be a major reason for the existence of the library and could well determine what periodicals should be cancelled. Only by keeping up with such activities can any library be sure that it is fulfilling its purpose.

In fact, it is often extemely difficult to match traditional resources and uses. As discussed by Charles Hamaker at the 1996 Charleston Conference, the use, even of an engineering collection, is largely by other users than those enrolled in the program.[8] Librarians have seldom brought together the various kinds of statistical information available to them, largely because the requisite statistical packages were not available. Circulation statistics are most often available, but require significant manipulation to relate them to the borrowers without violating the latter's privacy. Many libraries fail to maintain records of in-house use, even of bound volumes of serials. The importance of in-house uses is that they accumulate and derive from previous library actions, and thus provide libraries with a service program definition, together with some validation (or the reverse) of their collecting decisions. Unless librarians know whether their previous collecting decisions were valid, they have very little assurance that they can support more recent decisions.

Many years ago, one of the authors developed a series of library indicators, for use in a Planning, Programming, Budgeting Systems (PPBS) setting.[9] These may no longer be as valid as at that time but they do suggest ways in which libraries can evaluate their services in a financial manner, based as they were on both the cost and the need for specific transactions. The same is true of the 1996 study of New Zealand libraries by Coopers & Lybrand referred to earlier, which concentrates on output values and provides some ways of measuring them. Unless librarians are willing and able to define clearly their programs and their results, they will find it increasingly difficult to present cogent arguments for their financial support. There have been several endeavors to measure library performance but few of them have been able to relate closely to accounting principles. Although it is allowable that librarians should be concerned with the knowledge value of client transactions, they should also be concerned with their costs.

Library Programs

This is not the place to set out ideal program definitions. The intention here is, rather, to promote the idea of carefully examining what the library does so that each activity can be approached rationally to determine what its support needs are and how it relates to other library programs. For example, simply making a decision to cut back on serial subscriptions, no matter how necessary it may be in budget terms, is not enough to determine what the effects will be within the library and upon library users.[10] Attention should then be turned to the alternatives.

- Will these cuts result in more interlibrary loan requests?
- Will there be a rise in document delivery requests?
- Will there be more pressure on consortial members?
- Are there electronic substitutes available?
- If so, who will pay the associated costs?
- Is it possible to generate a fund to support document delivery?

This is the point at which libraries that have kept good records of internal usage will be in front of those that have not. Without some kind of knowledge of how the library's collection is being used and by whom, it is impossible to make intelligent collection decisions. Only too often, the decision is made to cancel "marginal" subscriptions, when more substantial savings could have been made by cancelling journals of record and substituting document delivery.[11] Further, the situation is complicated, especially for academic libraries, in that many of the faculty belong to the appropriate professional scholarly associations and therefore receive those societies' publications. As suggested by Charles Hamaker at the 1996 Charleston Acquisitions Conference, what people say they need is often very different from what they actually use[12], a finding that confirmed what appeared to be the case when the Boston Library Consortium attemped to reduce multiple holdings of serials.[13] There is little reason to assume that most people know what they want in detail or that they can explain it in library terms. Mostly they are uncertain of where they need to look or what kinds of information they need. This is the role of the librarian, to help guide users toward what they really need. Given this background, the library can look carefully at the kinds of interaction points provided and whether they actually meet user needs. Susan Zappen suggests, for example, that the shift from ownership to collaboration is not always beneficial,[14] and Linda Brown reminds us that:

> There may not be a single "right" way to set priorities for serials access and ownership. What's important is that priorities are set and articulated.[15]

The same methodology can be used to examine the reduction in reference points or changes in the number of items lent at one time. The need in both cases is to determine the effects on users, both absolutely and in terms of the patterns of use. In the former case, it may also be true that the library has some preconceptions that are invalid. Not all directional, informational, or reference questions are asked at the "reference" desk. Users may well prefer the informality of the circulation desk, or check at the catalog service desk if one is provided. While these kinds of transactions are somewhat outside the purview of this book, which is more concerned with changes in the resource budget, there are service changes directly related to resource budgeting that directly affect both reference and circulation services. In fact, librarians need to become more aware of the interactional nature of their client services. Reference and circulation result from collecting decisions, and reference queries may result in significant uses of both owned and accessed materials.

Information Access

In order to access electronic information library users must use one of the access points provided by the library. These are most often located within the reference department, or perhaps in the adult services area of a public library, and users will frequently require staff assistance. This kind of help is additional to any reference services provided under any earlier pattern and will, therefore, require extra staff or have to replace other services. Similarly, circulation departments may have to cope with handling requested materials where there is not already an interlibrary loan or document delivery department. In these ways movement toward resource or access budgeting spreads its influence throughout the library. The intermeshing of different library activities has become of prime importance in determining the ways in which a library budget can be cast. The acquisitions budget is no longer the prime determinant, even though reduced purchasing power has often spurred the development of alternative supply programs. As with program budgets, transaction budgets involve all expenditure sectors, albeit in differing proportions. Lest it be thought that only major reference questions involve a great deal of staff time, remember that helping a child or a parent find an appropriate picture or story book also takes a great deal of staff time and may well be equally productive in terms of the library's contribution to the local economy. It is all too easy to prejudge the value of any specific activity and too easy to downgrade it. To some extent, libraries have been following prevalent business philosophies in downgrading certain kinds of activity and in general downsizing. Whether all these assumptions applied in the library world was seldom asked. At the same time, the money available to most libraries failed to keep up with the rising prices of library materials, causing a library budget crisis.

Program Elements

While it may seem simple, at first sight, to identify the various elements in any specific program, it is often a quite complex procedure when, as in this context, we are looking at delivered products rather than at organizational divisions. In a way this means returning to the oldest budget format, the line-item budget, because it is necessary to identify all the portions of any transaction. While this may also seem to be the basis of the program or performance budget, there are subtle differences. The latter budgets are concerned with aggregate programs, each considered separately. The former is intended to produce some kind of comparative study so that the library, or other organization, can make choices between what activities to pursue.

There will always be some areas where there are no alternatives, for instance certain areas of interlibrary loan (see earlier chapters), and others where the institutional setting leads to a preference, for instance in the provision of reserve reading, or where the need to support a social good, such as children's reading, requires certain expenditures for which there are no substitutes. The transaction budget is also concerned with how well the library has fulfilled its "contract" with its users. It is concerned with user outcomes, though these may well be difficult to define, since only too often there is no direct response, or only a delayed one, to a library policy decision.

Program Analysis

The elements involved return to the three basics of all budgets, the elements that commingle in all programs. Though there are, as always, complexities in their definition and attribution, these are, briefly,

> Staff,
>
> Library materials, and
>
> Support expenditures (Other).

For many reasons, libraries have seldom analyzed staff expenditures in great detail, not because they do not want to, but because the time and effort did not seem justified. Then there is the issue of the various overheads:

> Supervision at all levels;
>
> Indirect costs, such as human resources;
>
> Backup computer services;
>
> Even something as simple as janitorial costs.

This kind of addition to program costs may seem excessive, but when a library is forced to look closely at those costs it is the only way to determine what they are. There will be differences between different kinds of libraries in the ways these costs are assessed, but it is clear that all libraries incur such costs.

One outstanding example of the lack of comprehensive data is the fact that many institutions do not include personal benefit costs in the individual budgets, which is one reason why the Association of Research Libraries has to point out that not all figures in its reports may be truly comparable. If setting up a particular operation involves highly paid professional staff, while another will only need middle level or clerical support, the exclusion or inclusion of benefit costs could lead to very different choices. These are the kinds of issues that will assume increasing importance in library budgeting, and they may well be joined by others as we become more experienced in handling the electronic information universe.

Benchmarking

There are also such issues as benchmarking.

- What is an appropriate workload for the department or the individual?
- How is this load determined?
- Are the comparative institutions appropriate?
- What is involved in each transaction?
- Where does it fit in the general workflow?
- Are there alternative measures?

Here one has to be very careful about the underlying assumptions. The nature of the work may vary widely from library to library, or even from department to department. For instance, handling rare books and similar materials is very different from handling current best-sellers. Even the outsourcing contract at the University of Alberta excluded rare books.[16] One case came to the authors' notice where the library was being downsized because its staff/circulation ratio was too high.[17] The staff were outraged and protested that many other factors had not been taken into account. The economic assumption that less is better is widespread but has very little justification, without a great deal more background investigation.

There is the need to differentiate between different kinds of information needs. The kinds of needs answered by special collections differ greatly from the kinds of questions that can be answered from general collections, and the resulting costs are significantly different. As libraries move collectively toward the digital preservation of published materials, the role of rare and special collections has to be given close attention. To some degree, special collections represent a decision to expend money on nonpopular or little-used material but they are also part of the greater need to ensure that such materials are preserved and available to future generations, an issue that has become increasingly more difficult in the age of electronic publishing. This may become even more important in the electronic future unless there are much more extensive agreements on protocols ensuring the integrity and the preservation of original electronic texts. Libraries should be aware that many major donors are interested in the preservation of the national intellectual heritage and want to help them to preserve the records of intellectual achievement. Unless libraries are willing to participate actively in the preservation of electronic materials, much that is essential to the understanding of our times may well simply vanish. Such activities are difficult to "benchmark," and may well fall outside the general library budget because they are tied up with consortial, state, or federal support.

Nevertheless, it makes good sense to try and arrive at some kinds of consistent measures to determine whether the library is acting sensibly or not.

How Professional Are Many Library Activities?

Similar economic assumptions are implicit in the clericalization of many library activities. It is often claimed that electronic information, such as databases, has made professional librarians less needed in interlibrary loan or circulation, but it has been forgotten (1) that many publications are not in the existing databases, and (2) that identifying any specific publication from incomplete or erroneous information may take much more than clerical knowledge. The importance of professional skills has been greatly downplayed, but the fact remains that only skilled librarians can recover difficult bibliographic information, calling on their own store of professional knowledge and experience.

These cases are cited to remind readers that it is necessary to compare like with like, and to understand differences before making comparisons. While it is easy to downplay the need for professional assistance, it is equally easy to overstate the role of nonprofessionals Given the increasing complexity of the information universe, libraries will have either to provide more local expertise or rely on outside sources.

Library Materials

The second major element of a budget relates to the library materials needed. In most library budgets it is difficult to relate the library materials budget directly to programs or services. While it may seem simpler in a public library, where the divisions are fewer, for example, children, young adult, adult, reference even these fall apart when it comes to using online resources, or even regular printed resources such as reference books. In academic libraries, there is a need to relate library materials purchases to academic programs as well as to see how they fit into library service programs. This more complex setting reflects the different community goals. When it becomes a matter of cancelling serials and substituting online access or document delivery, deriving program costs becomes even more difficult. The apparent nirvana of the virtual library has lulled many librarians into thinking that it is no longer important to decide what should be purchased or retained. Unfortunately the reality is that frequent consultation of online sources may cost far more than their direct purchase. It is still necessary to look at library materials as a primary program component, no matter whether these materials are printed or electronic.

In setting up any library program, the need for library materials in any format is a major concern, whether in print or other format, locally held or available elsewhere. If they cannot be provided readily, the program may well founder. Even with the vast promises of the various document delivery or information retrieval programs, there will always remain areas that cannot be readily supported. To a large extent traditional library programs intertwine. Purchase, interlibrary loan, and document delivery are likely to remain integral parts of any information delivery service for some time to come, supplemented by electronic access. Only by combining these elements into an efficient total delivery system can library clients' needs be met.

It is especially important to look at all aspects of electronic materials, since every use involves library costs. Though they are not taking up space on bookshelves, they are dependent on computer access, which uses substantial space,[18] and may need rather more intermediation than finding a book in the stacks. The needs of this kind of library are being explored tentatively in the new undergraduate library at the University of Southern California, where both printed materials and access to electronic information have been melded together, and the staff includes both librarians and computer experts.

Support Services

Any program or activity depends on other budget elements, such as computer access or printout capabilities. While some of these may seem quite direct, e.g., printing out a bibliography, others are inherent in the automated universe, such as software payments, hardware upgrades, or user payments. Libraries have to evaluate the support services they provide, whether in terms of photocopiers, programs for downloading information, or payments for the use of specific systems. These may seem truisms, but it has to be realized that most transactions involve different parts of the library and there may not be sufficient interaction to determine what changes are needed.

If a library decides to cancel subscriptions and rely on document delivery, the operation involved will need added support, or, alternatively, the library may seek to recover costs. The added support may mean added staff, newer equipment, or better space, but any of these conditions means added expenditure, whether or not some of that expenditure is recovered.

Financial Responsibility

The underlying budgetary consideration is who pays for what. For many years libraries have been seen as communal resources, not subject to specific, personal charges, nor plagued by questions regarding community and individual benefits. That setting has changed substantially as we have moved into a cost/benefit-related society. The questions now are not how to provide the best possible information but who should pay for what service. This has been accompanied by a wide range of economic approaches which attempt to determine the value of any indirect service. In this setting libraries must hover uncertainly between social services and economic boosters.

The Library in an Economic Context

Because these kinds of questions now relate to economic benefits to library users, the question of user payments looms large. How far can the library go in recovering its expenses in responding to individual needs which may have significant economic impact on the library's service community? Many libraries, both academic and public, have responded to this quandary by setting up fee-for-service activities, outside the regular library budget.[19] These services also relate to other changes in the information environment, especially those relating to copyright, but their principal concern is to transfer cost beneficial activities to a businesslike environment. The concern is that where there is a direct relationship to individual benefit the community should not be assessed with the cost. The contrary setting is where the individual benefit improves the community. The library is thus caught neatly in the middle and must evaluate all its services in terms of individual and community benefit. This conundrum is most specific for public libraries, which have traditionally not differentiated among their users, but who may now have to consider whether special services to a business client may be subject to income tax. Is the library acting as a business agent, or is it simply providing the kinds of services it would to any client? There are no easy answers, but libraries must clearly consider what their role is in relation to specific clients. The answers will differ according to the type of library involved, but cannot be avoided.

Social Issues

Librarians have to face the issue of how they can function in an environment that is much more concerned with financial survival than with informational and social needs. This leads to concern with who pays for what service, since payment relates to benefit.

- College and university librarians can often point out that information retrieval is an integral part of educational learning.
- Public librarians do not have such an escape point, but may be able to demonstrate that the service in question relates directly to their community goals.
- Special librarians have to demonstrate that such services are directly relevant to corporate intentions, or that the costs can and should be recovered directly from clients.

These statements, in themselves, indicate the wide range of social issues involved. Who benefits and who should pay are a primary concern. As suggested by Simmons and Hanks, there will always be the issue of equitable service. Will fees or other charges prevent users from gaining access to the information they need, and how should this be handled by a cooperative?[20] While most libraries regard their role as being in the public interest, there is always the nagging question of who benefitted directly. This in turn leads back to the consideration of who should pay for what services and how far the library is a public service. Public, in this sense, has a wide range of meanings, depending on who uses the library in question, but does not negate the need for financial wisdom. These considerations lead directly to the examination of transactional budgeting.

Transactional Budgeting

Transactional budgeting is a system based directly on the number and kinds of transactions taking place and the cost of each transaction. It is not exactly like the concerns of a retail establishment, which wishes to see what goods sell best, but rather is concerned with determining what mix of services will best meet public demand. In the library world, it seeks to determine what kinds of activities best meet its mission, quite apart from the fact that there may be charges involved in some settings. While it is admittedly difficult to determine the exact costs of specific activities, such as reference, the need is to determine the preponderant factors which favor one kind of response over another.

Transactional budgeting is done by assigning a price to any specific transaction and then comparing those prices to determine the most cost-effective response to a request. In library terms this means deconstructing the budget, to borrow a literary definition. In order to arrive at the most cost-effective way to respond to a user's requests, the library has to balance the costs and returns of using different retrieval methods. Since this may also be affected by any internal decisions on cost recovery, the process can be quite complex.

- Can the library, for example, guarantee the delivery (whether in the original or in computer simulated format) of the desired information?
- Must it use intermediaries to produce a set of responses, which must then be paid for?
- Would it be necessary to develop a complete set of references, which would then, in turn, need to be investigated, at further cost?
- What is the effect of involving several intermediaries?
- Can these intermediaries reduce the total cost?

While these questions may seem marginal, in the age of electronic information they are becoming crucial, because they define the ways in which information is obtained. What we are looking at is the set of transactions involved in evaluating specific library-user interactions.

The concept of transactional budgeting involves some degree of knowledge of the costs involved in each transaction. To date, the library community has provided little such data other than in relation to interlibrary loan.[21] This situation must change so that it can become clearer what costs are involved in circulation, acquisition, and reference, for example, and, on a larger scale, what are the costs and benefits of cooperation. There have been some studies of acquisition and cataloging procedures, but none as comprehensive as in the case of interlibrary loan. Unless librarians can feel confident that they can assign costs to each kind of transaction, their budgetary basis will continue to be uncertain. Even further, there is the need to establish costs for document delivery. If costs are being recovered, librarians need to know what those costs are so that, at the least, they can justify them to their users. This is true of any library transaction, even so apparently simple a one as borrowing a book.

Fees and Charges

In today's library, it is difficult to decide what activities are involved, let alone what kinds of services should be charged for or free. Librarians, therefore, have to look carefully at their environments:

- What is provided as a public or community good?
- What is regarded as a personal service to be paid for?

The balance between these two goods may well tax the intelligence of any librarian. If the information in question is publicly accessible and free, how can the library charge, even though it has to support the general costs of providing computers, software, and downloading and printing. If it is proprietorial, there may well be justification for passing on access costs.

When the time comes for a library to move toward transactional budgeting, and this may well be the result of having to respond to calls for cost recovery in cases of individual benefit, it becomes necessary to determine how to develop charges for individual transactions and ways in which to recover some or all of such costs.[22] There are no totally adequate paradigms, but it should be possible to apply general accounting principles, and it may be necessary to incorporate much finer measuring tools than are commonly used. The most important aspect of this approach is that it seeks to place each kind of library response in context and assign both a value and a cost to it. Unless this is done, it is virtually impossible to determine what portions of the library budget should be assigned to acquisition, access, interlibrary loan, or document delivery. The need to do so has become overwhelming, since most financial sources have now become much more wary about supporting activities that do not show a direct financial return.

Summary

Libraries now face much more complex budget issues than deciding how much money to allocate to materials, to staff, and to other expenditures. Most library transactions now involve all three factors, often in differing degrees. The basic need is to decide how to allocate the library budget to meet the differing information access needs. The secondary decision is what, if any, services should be charged back to library users.

Notes   1. For an examination of this concept in relation to libraries see "Responsibility Centered Management and the University Library" by James G. Neal and Lynn Smith, *Bottom Line* 8, no. 4 (1995): 17–20. For a more complete institutional examination see *Responsibility Centered Budgeting,* by E. L. Whalen (Bloomington: Indiana University Press, 1991).

2. The library literature abounds with news items relating to the problems faced by the San Francisco Public Library following its move to expand electronic services. There were questions relating to the disposition of discarded library materials, the move to provide information to local government and business on a cost basis, and whether the library, as a tax-supported institution, could undertake such measures. These fundamental library service issues have been obscured by concern about budget overrides, which were virtually inevitable for a library that was truly seeking to respond to the new information age. In fact, very few public authorities have begun to comprehend the costs involved in going electronic.

3. Coopers & Lybrand, *Valuing the Economic Costs and Benefits of Libraries: A Study Prepared for the N Strategy* (Wellington: New Zealand Library & Information Association, 1996); and Nancy A. Van House, Beth T. Weil, and Charles R. McClure, *Measuring Academic Library Performance: A Practical Approach* (Chicago: American Library Association, 1990).

4. John M. Budd, "A Critique of Customer and Commodity," *College & Research Libraries* 58, no. 4 (July 1997): 310–21.

5. Jane P. Kleiner and Charles A. Hamaker, "Libraries 2000: Transforming Libraries Using Document Delivery, Needs Assessment, and Networked Resources," *College & Research Libraries* 58, no. 4 (July 1997): 355–74.

6. Robert Lent, Louise A. Buckley, and David Lane, "Money Talks But Can It Listen?—How We Found Out What Our Faculty Really Read," *Against the Grain* 9, no. 2 (April 1997): 1, 16, 18, 20, 34.

7. Linda Mielke, "Short-Range Planning for Turbulent Times," *American Libraries* 26, no. 9 (October 1995): 905–6.

8. Charles Hamaker at the 1996 Charleston Acquisitions Conference following his presentation on serials cancellations at the Louisiana State University library.

9. Murray S. Martin, *Budgetary Control in Academic Libraries* (Greenwich, Conn.: JAI Press, 1978). Several references, but see especially pp. 69–74.

10. Susan B. Ardis and Karen B. Croneis, "Document Delivery, Cost Containment, and Serial Ownership," *College & Research Library News,* 48 (November 1987): 624–27.

11. Tina E. Chrzatowski and Karen A. Schmidt, "Collections at Risk: Revisiting Serial Cancellations in Academic Libraries," *College & Research Libraries* 57, no. 4 (July 1996): 351–64; and "Surveying the Damage: Academic Library Serial Cancellations 1987–88 through 1989–90," *College & Research Libraries* 54, no. 2 (March 1993): 92–102.

12. Jane P. Kleiner and Charles A. Hamaker, "Libraries 2000." There are other studies cited in the bibliography which suggest that more research is needed into the relationship between serial cancellations, library budgets, and information recovery.

13. From personal experience, the chemistry faculty at Tufts University were reluctant to cancel any subscriptions even when it was possible to demonstrate that the titles in question had not been used in over a year. This suggests the chasm between user and librarian perception of the need for information. Further, it was impossible to switch from the paper to the electronic version of *Chemical Abstracts* because a teaching program had been set up which required students to search the paper version for citations.

14. Susan H. Zappen, "From Cancellation to Collaboration—Some Thoughts," *Against the Grain* 9, no. 3 (June 1997): 1, 16, 68+.

15. Linda A. Brown, "Balancing Information Needs with Serials Values and Costs," *Against the Grain* 9, no. 2 (April 1997): 22–24, 26, 28.

16. Murray S. Martin and Ernie Ingles, "Outsourcing in Alberta," *Bottom Line* 8, no. 4 (1995): 32–34.

17. The reference is to the Wellington Public Library (New Zealand) in a local newspaper. "Librarians 'Disoriented' by Change," by Jane Collins, *City Voice*.

18. It has been suggested by Geoffrey Freeman, in a personal communication, that the average electronic work station will occupy 50 square feet, substantially more than has usually been allowed for a reading station.

19. *Fiscal Currents,* a publication of the Fee Based Services to Academic Libraries Discussion Group (Association of College and Research Libraries), reports on these activities and provides substantial information on how to organize such library activities.

20. R. Simmons and G. Hanks, "Equitable Non-Resident Fees Are Critical in the Provision of Library Services for All Idahoans," *Idaho Librarian* 47 (July 1995): 82.

21. Marilyn M. Roche, *ARL/RLG Interlibrary Loan Cost Study: A Joint Effort by the Association of Research Libraries and the Research Libraries Group* (Washington, D.C.: ARL, 1993).

22. Murray S. Martin and Betsy Park, *Setting Fees and Fines: A How-to-Do-It Manual for Librarians* (New York: Neal-Schuman, 1997).

11

Choosing Alternative Information Sources

The basic issue in transactional budgeting, which we see as being basic to library budgets in the future, is looking at the various costs and benefits associated with any specific mode of information delivery and making choices between them in determining how best to meet each demand for information. The budget implications of each choice may not now easily be determined, because we do not have sufficient financial information available, but libraries should strive to meet this goal. There are three parts in any information transaction: the requester, the provider (the library in this case), and the information itself. The goal in any such transaction is to ensure that the information flows as easily as possible from the provider to the requester.

At the simplest level, this correlates with charging out a book to an individual borrower. At its most complex, it may involve searching through many electronic files, determining which, if any, has the needed information, and then downloading or copying it. The library is the intermediary in both kinds of transaction, but what it does and what its actions cost may differ significantly from one transaction to another. This is why libraries, faced with demands to cover their service costs to nonlocal users or for special activities, need to be able to show what each kind of activity involves. As Tilson suggests, this kind of income-generation is becoming more widespread in England,[1] a situation paralleled in New Zealand.[2] The same drive lies behind the establishment of fee-for-service operations in public and academic libraries throughout the United States, though these latter tend to be concerned with service to external patrons rather than internal users. This may not always be the case with document delivery services, as pointed out in chapter 8. Each kind of source chosen has its own financial implications, and the final mix determines the whole library budget. Choosing between these sources, therefore, is a matter of great importance, and requires direct attention by all library staff and managers.

Interlibrary Loan and Its Budget Implications

The purpose of interlibrary loan is to transfer specific publications from one library to another for the benefit of the receiving library's patrons. Simple as this may seem, it conceals a wide range of transactions and their accompanying costs. First, there is the cost of the library staff involved. While this is common to all library transactions, it is most marked in this kind of transaction where the library may well have to invest a considerable amount of staff time in its completion. Second, there is the cost of transmittal, usually considered a wash since there are reciprocal actions by other libraries, but the cost of postage, delivery service, sometimes photocopying, can be considerable. There may be payments relating to copyright, especially in international transactions, and transactions with Canada may also be subject to general sales tax. Third, there may be the need to supervise the use of the materials so provided and to guarantee that they are returned in the same condition they were received. This may seem picayune, but we have known cases in which books have been virtually destroyed by photocopying even though the lending library had strictly forbidden such usage.

The Cost of Interlibrary Loan

The budget implications are clear. Any interlibrary loan transaction will be costly. The present best estimates place these costs in the range of $20 to $25 for both the requesting and the receiving library. Costs will differ considerably by type and size of library, with smaller libraries unlikely to reach such levels. Nevertheless, the library has to determine whether interlibrary loan falls within freely provided services or should be subject to some kind of fee or recovery charge. In some instances, this may have been predetermined by a state or other agency that has ruled against charging any fee.[3] This is most likely to be true for public libraries, but publicly supported academic libraries may also be affected, and in other academic libraries it may be considered an essential scholarly service.

Electing to use interlibrary loan to meet a patron's need sets in train this sequence of costs, and libraries have to decide whether they can include these in their regular operating costs or set up a cost recovery mechanism. Interlibrary loan is a relatively costly library operation because it involves expensive staff time and expensive operating costs. It may, however, be the only answer to any specific request. On the other hand, it may often be seen as a way to reduce patron reliance on the budget for materials. This is a logistical error, since the costs, in either setting, will fall within the library's ambit, and it will become necessary to determine who pays, the library or the user?

Information Access and Interlibrary Loan

Following the many serial cancellation projects that have marked the current academic library situation,[4] interlibrary loan was usually seen as the alternative. Unfortunately, the administrators who supported this change in direction were not fully aware of the costs associated with the shift.[5] They either overestimated the ability of their staffs to respond or underestimated the costs of that response. Interlibrary loan will undoubtedly continue to be the response when a library patron needs to read a whole book or a similar printed publication, but may well be superseded by document delivery or electronic access in the case of articles or electronic publications. In all settings, however, attention has to be paid to the medium the needed information inhabits. It makes no sense to use the Internet for direct access to printed materials, and many databases are not accessible simply on demand. Thus, interlibrary loan is likely to retain a major role well into the next century, despite the advocates of electronic access.

The first requirement, seldom explored, is to determine what effects serial cancellations and similar collection adjustments will have on interlibrary loan and parallel activities. A similar result may derive from the use of databases.[6] If, as might be expected, the need for borrowing grows, then the library will need to spend more on its interlibrary loan operations. These effects are not necessarily at all clear. There need be little or no relationship between the cancelled titles and the articles requested,[7] and databases will open a much wider range of titles to the user, including many the library would never have considered purchasing in the first place. Similarly, libraries need to check carefully the relationship between their own holdings and the contents of the databases in question. In some cases, it is possible to tag the records for local ownership, which would both improve information retrieval for the user and increase local use.

There may be need for more staff, for better equipment, e.g., Ariel technology, and the need for decisions about whether or not to charge, or whether to set up some kind of revolving fund, for example, to support student use. In any event, the ILL budget will need to be strengthened to cover not only added out-of-pocket expenses but also added costs. Certainly interlibrary loan will continue to be needed for the borrowing of complete books, and probably for articles from periodicals covered by "fair use" (though it remains important to stress that a subscription for a frequently needed journal is certainly going to be cheaper than either interlibrary loan or document delivery), but also for obtaining materials from other countries that do not have the appropriate electronic connections.

Libraries must, then, determine how many of their off-site transactions should be handled by interlibrary loan and how many by other library agencies. These decisions need to be based on the respective ability of the various means of delivery to effect a successful conclusion to the transaction. The resulting decisions will undoubtedly affect the distribution of budgetary expenditures.

Document Delivery and Its Budget Implications

Document delivery is too often seen as the answer to patrons' needs for materials the library does not own. This decision automatically brings the library into the struggle between information producers and consumers as to who should pay for what. Whereas interlibrary loan, conducted with due regard to legal considerations, does not involve the library in the payment of royalties or similar fees, document delivery, which is mostly conducted with the assistance of commercial or quasi-commercial firms, will automatically raise the issue of such payments, some of which can be substantial. It also requires the hiring of dedicated staff, even if only on a part-time basis (or the part-time allocation of existing staff), and the purchase or rental of dedicated equipment and services in order not to detract from other services.

- Is such a move cost-effective?
- Does it meet all the local service criteria?

Librarians have tended to skirt these issues. Setting up fee-based services seemed to distance the library from the need to contemplate charges for its other services. Gradually, however, the growth of document delivery services has tended to reduce the difference. Moreover, many academic librarians in the wake of various judicial decisions decided that it was easier to pay whatever royalties were required for reserve copies than to endure the problems of a major lawsuit. The back-off attitude may be somewhat more difficult after such legal actions as the *Texaco* case regarding photocopying for various branch libraries, even though that was settled out of court. The other issues relating to document delivery are the ways in which such costs as copying and delivery are assessed and charged. Many libraries have produced schedules of charges for such services, and it is sometimes difficult to determine whether interlibrary loan or document delivery is either the cheaper or the more effective service.[8] Some libraries have used money recouped from the cancellation of serials to support document delivery, but such actions still beg the question of fiscal responsibility for the entire range of services offered by the library.

Whatever the decision, anyone contemplating document delivery on a wide scale will have to look closely at how the operation is set up and financed. To preserve its not-for-profit status any library would be well advised not to combine document delivery and interlibrary loan, since the latter operates under special copyright provisions while the former is subject to other kinds of legal controls as a quasi-business. This suggests that librarians will need to segment their operations into for-profit and not-for-profit activities, and then decide what kinds of activities fall into either category.

Electronic Access and Its Budget Implications

Because it seems relatively easy to obtain access to electronic information, those in charge of library budgets need to consider the many kinds of costs associated with such access and whether these costs can be assigned to individual users or to the general cost of the library system. The slow development of Internet access, and the reluctance of many publishers to enter the business of electronic publishing while the rules about costs and charges are still unclear, suggests that the growth of this factor in library budgets will be somewhat slow. As Bailey suggests, there are so many unsettled matters that the growth of regularly published material on the Internet will be uneven, though there will be a growth of direct publishing, albeit without the kinds of controls generally associated with academic publishing.[9] These concerns about controls are not groundless, since it is possible simply to change or delete without consultation any materials on the Internet. Librarians still have to be concerned about the ways in which they can provide their users with the most up-to-date information, whatever the format.

Library Responsiveness

Librarians must, however, begin to determine how to provide such information. Their determinations will depend on a wide variety of legal and commercial decisions not yet made, and, for the most part, not yet even contemplated. If it is finally decided that there will be a per-view charge (similar to a charge for browsing in a bookstore!) that would instantly create an entirely different information world.[10] In these circumstances librarians should be wary of any unauthorized forays into the world of electronic information. Of particular importance is the difference between accessing a book and accessing electronic media referred to by Charles Bailey, because the first is a simple matter of picking up something that has already been purchased and is therefore subject to the Doctrine of First Sale, while the second is like accessing a datafile that is not in the public domain. There are future possibilities like encryption, which will automatically trigger either charges or eviction from the file, and it may also be possible to place the entire file in some encoded format so that only those with permission, usually paid for, can access it. In such a setting we are dealing with privileged information, available to only one person at a time for that person's retention, and libraries have to consider seriously whether they can or should provide free public access. The alternative may be charging for each use or passing on the various costs incurred. This, in turn, raises some very real social concerns.

- Can such charges eliminate information service for those who cannot pay?
- Can the library subsidize some users and not others?
- Which sets of users fall into either class?

It will be some time still before these problems are resolved, but librarians, in the meantime, will have to look closely at how they provide and pay (or charge) for electronic access. Access, in this sense, includes all monitoring of a document whether printed or electronic, since "reading" or "browsing" an electronic document not owned by the library will almost certainly trigger some direct charge.

Purchase and Its Budget Implications

The purchase by a library of any material, whether printed, recorded, or electronic, carries with it an overhead of certain legal considerations. Under the Doctrine of First Sale, further use by library patrons is not subject to any royalty. It is true that many electronic packages carry with them directives about use, often triggered by simply opening the plastic seal, but it is not so clear whether these are in fact actual legal restrictions or simply an attempt to prevent expanded use. This issue is discussed in more detail in chapter 9. Generally, however, once a library has bought something, its further use is a matter between the library and its patrons, and there is also the ability to share with other libraries.

The other kinds of implications are the use of library funds to provide reading or reference materials which then become a permanent capital expenditure, even though they may have been purchased from operating revenues. Because most responsible authorities have found it far beyond their capacity to monitor and record the purchase of individual books at relatively minor prices, they have tended to leave this to the library—and perhaps the institution's insurers—so that there is no clear body of institutional practice to decide whether "books" are indeed capital purchases. It is noteworthy, however, that there are many examples of rules for their disposal which suggest that, in some fashion, they are regarded as capital purchases. It is possible to demonstrate that, after years of purchasing library materials, libraries have, in fact, constructed the most valuable capital asset on campus or in the town, and that it should be so regarded, meaning that it is appropriate to expend money to maintain its capital value.

For many years, library standards tended to suggest some kinds of ratios for library materials expenditures as against personnel and operating expenditures. With the changes in the learning environment that have been taking place, the Standards for University Libraries produced by the Association of College and Research Libraries began to move in a different direction, emphasizing services and user response.[11] Although this has not yet become totally acceptable to the library community, more recent studies concentrating on performance rather than acquisition have reinforced the need for a new approach to library service.[12] While purchased materials will continue to remain important, access and document delivery will also share the stage, increasingly so as the publishing community or individual authors take on this new approach.

One of the less studied aspects of library service is the cost of purchasing materials. With the growth of outsourcing this is becoming much more important in budget terms. In fact, however, many academic libraries have been outsourcing for years via the many standing order plans available, nationally and internationally. These have undoubtedly reduced the cost per item of obtaining printed materials, but have raised other issues relating to international and nontrade publishing where standard purchasing procedures are often less effective and librarians have to search for special contacts, including the possibility of exchanging publications. The further examination of outsourcing (in a series of workshops at the ALA Midwinter in Washington in 1997) has suggested that dealers may use totally inappropriate factors in deciding on what materials to supply.[13] Despite these problems, the outsourcing of some or all library operations is likely to continue. It may well reduce the costs of acquisition and processing, but may not be able to do any better in the matter of claims for unsupplied books, unless the problems noted by Arlene Sievers at the 1991 Charleston Acquisitions Conference can be addressed and overcome.[14] Although this factor has not been directly addressed in the recent debate, it is worth noting that, if there is only one party engaged in both selecting and ordering, there will be no way to determine whether a wanted book was ordered or was actually available.

Contracted Services and Their Budget Implications

For many years libraries have contracted with vendors to provide services. For the most part these have related to the purchase and provision of printed materials. We are now, however, facing a setting where vendors can contract to supply other kinds of services, such as access to electronic information. To a large extent, such contracts offer libraries reduced costs if their use meets a certain minimum. If not, they may have to pay extra charges. Sometimes these contracts are negotiated through a consortium, which then assumes the costs associated with the contract, but these remain dependent on the amount of money involved. An example of this would be a group of libraries contracting to maintain an online database consisting of all the ISI *Current Contents* periodicals, which would include both savings from canceling paper subscriptions and the benefits of a good rate on electronic copies. Another prime example is the OHIOlink/Elsevier contract for the electronic supply of all Elsevier titles, mediated for individual libraries by the Ohio consortium. The cost remains roughly the equivalent of the total then-exisitng subscriptions, but the benefits become more widespread and equalized. In these and in all similar situations both parties have to take care to safeguard their economic, legal, and social concerns. Someone has to pay for any contracted services, and any library contemplating such action is well advised to examine carefully all the details of any proposal and to seek legal advice. It may well be the preferred option, but the way in which it is set up and controlled can have wide financial repercussions for the library.

Library Status

Because libraries generally operate as nonprofit entities, librarians have to be concerned that they do not undertake activities that could threaten this status and force them to file income returns with the IRS. Document delivery services may well fall within the realm of income-producing activities and should, therefore, be separated financially from all other library activities. This may simply be an accounting procedure, but librarians should be aware that the assignment of costs and profits to the operation may be very difficult if it is not entirely separated from other library operations. Here the issue is less the level of service provided than the relationship between the provider and the receiver. While most public librarians would maintain that their relationships with patrons seeking information are simply between library and patron, there are many issues that move far beyond library/user relationships. In many settings the library services involved approximate the kinds of services that would be provided by a corporate library and would therefore seem to be paid-for services. If any library acts to help a corporate client, such an action could be construed as profit-motivated. While this may not, in fact, be the case, appearances may suggest a contrary interpretation. This becomes even more pressing with the advent of electronic information services, because the library's transactions are likely to be recorded by a third party, and because the Internet is becoming much more commercialized.

The problem faced by librarians is the degree to which their activities can be regarded as tax-exempt, which means that they must look closely at all transactions. If they seem to be profit related, they may have to be abstracted from all other library transactions and placed in a separate budget that may be subject to some kind of tax. This is not easy to do and requires extensive familiarity with IRS regulations, usually far beyond most librarians' expertise.

Summary

Libraries must now look closely at the ramifications of their transactions. While it was simple to look at book and serial purchases and see the library as a go-between for publisher and user, the same is no longer true in the electronic age. Where the library seeks to provide printouts or downloaded information, there may be added copyright considerations. In addition, the cost of accessing and transferring electronic information is substantially higher than even the cost of photocopying, and there are much wider copyright considerations. Even if it is possible for a library to sign up for an access program, it is likely that it will involve substantial costs, which the library may or may not want to recover from its users. Further, contractual services raise many more issues of fiscal responsibility, and libraries may well have to look at the effects on their nonprofit status.

Notes

1. Yvette Tilson, "Income Generation and Pricing in Libraries," *Bottom Line: Managing Library Finances* 8, no. 2 (1995): 23–36.

2. There are numerous references to this kind of situation in *Library Life Te Rau Ora* (the newsletter of the New Zealand Library and Information Association) and the issue for June 1997 (213, p. 13) contains a preliminary statement of the application of the cost/benefit principles developed by Coopers & Lybrand in relation to the library of the New Zealand Dairy Board.

3. Pete Giacoma, *The Fee or Free Decision: Legal, Economic, Political, and Ethical Perspectives for Public Libraries* (New York: Neal-Schuman, 1989). See Appendix 1 for a summary of state laws and regulations, and discussions elsewhere. Some legislation may have been changed since the time of writing.

4. Tina E. Chrzatowski and Karen A. Schmidt, "Collections at Risk: Revisiting Serial Cancellations in Academic Libraries," *College & Research Libraries* 57, no. 4 (July 1996): 351–64; and "Surveying the Damage: Academic Library Serial

Cancellations 1987–88 through 1989–90," *College & Research Libraries* 54, no. 2 (March 1993): 92–102.

5. Marilyn M. Roche, *ARL/RLG Interlibrary Loan Cost Study: A Joint Effort by the Association of Research Libraries and the Research Libraries Group* (Washington, D.C.: ARL, 1993). While this study is by no means definitive and may apply only to a specific kind of library, it certainly opened wide the issue of what both borrowing and lending libraries paid to support ILL transactions. Similar studies of document delivery are overdue.

6. Jody Bates Foote and Roland C. Reson, "The Unexpected Effect of Online Databases on Undergraduate Use of Interlibrary Loan," *Journal of Interlibrary Loan, Document Delivery & Information Supply* 5, no. 4 (1995): 65–72.

7. Jane P. Kleiner and Charles A. Hamaker, "Libraries 2000: Transforming Libraries Using Document Delivery, Needs Assessment, and Networked Resources," *College & Research Libraries* 58, no. 4 (July 1997): 355–74.

8. Wayne Pederson and David Gregory, "Interlibrary Loan and Commercial Document Supply: Finding the Right Fit," *Journal of Academic Librarianship* 20, no. 5/6 (November 1994): 263–72.

9. A useful survey of this problem is provided by Charles W. Bailey Jr. in "Bricks, Bytes, or Both? The Probable Impact of Scholarly Electronic Publishing on Library Space Needs," in *Information Imagineering: Meeting at the Interface,* ed. Milton T. Wolf, Pat Ensor, and Mary Augusta Thomas (Chicago: American Library Association, 1998): 89–99.

10. *Intellectual Property and the National Information Infrastructure: The Report of the Working Group on Intellectual Property Rights,* Bruce A. Lehman, Chair (Washington, D.C.: U.S. Department of Commerce, 1995).

11. Association of College and Research Libraries, "Standards for University Libraries: Evaluation of Performance," *College & Research Libraries News* (September 1989): 679–91.

12. Performance standards are not generally available for most kinds of libraries, although there has been some movement toward evaluating performance, and studies such as that by Coopers & Lybrand prepared for the New Zealand Library and Information Association appear to set up performance standards.

13. These references are basically to the total outsourcing program in Hawaii, and are scattered through several library periodicals. Some striking cases are cited by Sheila Intner in her editorial "Stream of Consciousness: Outsourcing Selection in Hawaii—The Next Installment," *Technicalities* 17, no. 4 (April 1997): 2–3. It is worth noting, however, that other libraries have entered into outsourcing contracts, notably the Riverside County (California) Public Library, which signed a two-year deal with Library Systems and Services, Inc., of Germantown, Maryland, for the complete operation of the system's twenty-five branches, though there will be an advisory board and a project director (*Library Journal* 122, no. 12 (July 1997): 12).

14. Arlene Moore Sievers, "Books in Limbo: Book Distribution and Supply Problems that Affect Academic Libraries," in *Issues in Collection Management: Librarians, Booksellers, Publishers,* ed. Murray S. Martin (Greenwich, Conn.: JAI Press, 1995).

12

Changing from Purchase to Contracts and Leases

Librarians have traditionally based their library materials budgets on purchasing materials required by their users. Gradually, however, alternatives have begun invading that budget. Electronic information providers have found it increasingly advantageous to use either contracts or leases to cover the library use of their products. One of the major but little mentioned reasons for this is that most of the contents of such compilations or databases are not subject to copyright but are in the public domain. Under any purchase agreement, the library could make unlimited use of the database. Of course, this statement overlooks the intellectual and financial investment in creating the database, but the provider is thus forced to look for other ways to recoup development costs. In these situations nothing changed hands as it did with a purchase, but the lessee or contractee had to abide by whatever conditions were established. With the growth of electronic publications and services, this kind of relationship has expanded rapidly and librarians now find themselves as much involved in negotiating leases and contracts as with simple purchase. In fact, the involvement may even be greater when it becomes necessary to consult lawyers and other specialists about the terms of a contract or lease. It may turn out that the library is obligated to pay a basic fee regardless of use or that each use incurs some kind of overhead. There may be provisions about how the information is to be used or shared, and the library may well turn out to be the middleman in a wide range of transactions. All these situations affect the library's budget and its distribution.[1]

Control of Electronic Connections

Unless steps are taken to monitor and control the library's participation in electronic networks, it may become subject to a wide variety of costs that were never anticipated. This does not need to mean diminished service to library users. It may, however, mean a different distribution of information access costs between user and library.

The library's response to information access costs will differ according to its mission.

- Public libraries are seldom in the position to pick up incidental information access costs, and may not be able under controlling legislation to levy charges for a service deemed regular or normal, such as reference, even over the telephone.
- Academic libraries may be caught in a major bind. The institution's administration wants its students and faculty to be in a leading information position, but may not always be able to provide the necessary budget support. In this setting, where are user charges appropriate, and where not? Most academic libraries have long since levied charges for photocopy, and many have now begun to look at their financial responsibilities in other information-sharing procedures.
- Special libraries, while still having to be aware of cost overruns, have the ability to charge back search costs either to the individual being served or to the research project in question, as distinct from the wider needs of public and academic libraries.

These differences in mission and response lie behind the somewhat muddled library response to the recent massive changes in the information universe. Unless libraries and information providers can negotiate their differences, the future seems to be riddled with uncertainty, which militates against the best interests of both parties, not to mention the actual end-user. As indicated in other chapters, libraries must now look at their services in terms of what they provide for the user, rather than in terms of collection size.

Electronic Access

The issue here is that, as distinct from access to printed materials, access to electronic materials appears both simpler and more direct, though there is no assurance that such will always be the case. Transactional costs have not been fully developed and need a lot more attention. They involve all segments of the library budget, but libraries have seldom arrived at a transaction-based charge for such use. At most they charge back any direct costs, except in a fee-for-service setting. This attitude derives from the tradition of free library service, which may no longer be the ruling concept in an electronic universe.

Traditional library usage seldom involved more than the borrowing of owned printed materials or the consultation of other printed reference sources. Such uses were relatively inexpensive and did not involve the library other than marginally. Now that the universe has expanded to include online information, databases, and similar sets of data, libraries have to look more carefully at how they respond to individual user needs.[2] These needs have now widened, especially with all the attention that is being focused on the Internet, and requests may now also be received online or via the telephone, which means they can come from anywhere. Some libraries have sought to charge for telephone reference, but many public libraries are unable to do so, because their governing legislation does not allow it. The rules surrounding the provision and receipt of information may well need to be redrawn.

Photocopy and Electronics: Similarities and Differences

As photocopying expanded, libraries found they had to develop newer service protocols and charge mechanisms.[3] The process expanded exponentially as it became possible to consult and download, or print out electronic information. Libraries then had to consider whether the rather simple rules applying to photocopy could be applied equally to electronic transactions. Whereas photocopying dealt with owned resources, downloading deals with leased or accessed resources, and the rules are totally different. This change has been explored extensively in the report of an Association of Research Libraries conference, which looked at the changes inherent in a shift from print to electronics.[4] As could be expected, in this setting, purchase practice and law, contract law and its effects, and the legal settings surrounding leases and consultation may have far-reaching effects. The pace of change has been so rapid that this report is already somewhat out of date, but it does set out the continuing problems relating to the provision of academic information, and, by extension, the provision of information to the community at large.

The simple solutions available in the age of print are no longer so readily available in the electronic age. Not only do libraries have to determine what rights their direct users may have, but what responses they have to make to other would-be users, whose access comes via a totally new range of electronic sources. The rights and needs of nonlocal users have not yet been subject to extensive scrutiny, largely because electronic access to any one library is still a novel experience and there are no guidelines for handling such access. Do users from another country, for example, have the same rights to access information? To some extent this issue was sidelined when the bulk of those seeking information were librarians or users from other American libraries, but since it has become possible for the whole world to have access, the stakes have changed.

The Players in the Information Game

Although librarians have always thought of publishers and authors as participants in the provision of information, they have seldom looked directly at the roles that each must play. There are now added participants in the form of software and hardware vendors, electronic gateways, service vendors (akin to book and serial vendors), and a wide range of independent consultants, all prepared to render service in return for payment. Some of these are like wholesale vendors, others are more like retail vendors, and some are only interested in providing a bridge between user and provider.

It is not surprising that librarians are becoming confused as to how they should respond to this rapidly widening series of commercial relationships. It is of special importance that these new concerns involve a wide range of legal issues, which require a totally different kind of response than was appropriate in the days when the sole matter of concern was printed materials.[5] Libraries are now operating in an only partially defined information arena, where the participants and the providers have taken on new roles. To some extent the library has even been bypassed, as people work directly with online vendors and use credit cards or set up their own accounts. Whether they achieve the same level of success is not a question that is easily asked or answered. Judging, however, by the increasing need for instruction in the use of a complex and confusing source, it would seem that librarians and libraries are still needed.

Outsourcing

Although the outsourcing of a library's purchasing program is not the direct interest of this book, it clearly has implications for collection development. Any library so involved must think carefully about what the results will be. We have heard at length about problems relating to local responsibilities.[6] So far, we have heard less about the benefits, which may be substantial, so long as the profile on which the vendor is acting is appropriate, something academic libraries have been doing for decades. One of the major academic outsourcing programs, instituted by the University of Alberta, seems to have been very successful,[7] but a major factor there was the establishment of a library surveillance committee to ensure the maintenance of quality service. Although libraries have always outsourced some of their activities, especially binding, and the majority of actual library purchasing has long been carried out by vendors and similar library agents, the reaction to outsourcing selection, cataloging, and processing has reached mega-decibel levels, without any significant attempt to explain why. As Robert Renaud suggests, libraries need to learn how to compete in the information world, where roles are currently only partially defined.[8]

In part, it represents the reaction of traditional librarians, who see their control of libraries challenged, but it also suggests that there may be even larger concerns related to user need. As Betty Eddison has pointed out, our profession is changing and needs to be much more concerned with the role of the librarian.[9] How far any library program should be truly local and how far it should reflect even larger interests remain a matter for much more discussion. Much of the rapid growth of library collections in the '70s and '80s could not have happened without the assistance of publishers and dealers in the development of blanket orders and similar programs. It would be very unfortunate indeed if that kind of cooperation should be overtaken by a time when the general relationship is one of carping and criticism. This criticism is not one-sided. So far publishers and software vendors have taken a very hard line over copyright and seem unwilling to come to any compromise agreement with libraries. Some such agreement is essential if both publishers and libraries are to maintain their roles within the information universe.

Library-Publisher Relations

Following a long period of harmonious cooperation, libraries and publishers appear to have moved apart. One of the principal causes seems to be a growing difference over copyright, based principally on libraries' use of interlibrary loan rather than document delivery. The legal issues here are indeed complex, but no one has yet proved conclusively that interlibrary loan has materially harmed publishers, especially if it is carried out within the CONTU guidelines. To some extent, the shrinking of library acquisition budgets has contributed to this perception, but, even if all borrowing and lending activities between libraries were charged back to library users and included copyright payments, there would still not be enough in most library budgets to enable them to buy everything they either want or need. Since, at the same time, these budgets are being used to support electronic access, the library is caught in a double bind. Even the few examples of cooperative projects, mostly the building of full-text serial databases, can do little to relieve the strain on the budget. They may, however, add emphasis to the apparent privatization of access to information.

Contracts

As distinct from purchases, contracts for service, whether from primary or secondary providers, are subject to different legal standards. Libraries engage to pay for services from publishers or database vendors, in much the same way as they would have to contract for any outside services. For the most part this relates to the provision of databases or online searches, but it is clear that, with the growth of the Internet, it may well include reference and similar services, as well as the right to consult or download specific publications. An instance of the latter is the latest proposed online version of the *Encyclopaedia Britannica,* where there would be a charge for each use. The question facing all libraries is whether to pass on these costs to their users, since the library has no inherent property right in the information in question. This may not be quite so in certain instances, where the library has actually paid in advance for use, or where the contract allows for specified kinds of use without charge, but the general issue remains.

Because libraries have no track record in this area, it will undoubtedly take some time to develop guidelines or governing principles. The very idea that an individual library might be able to participate in global information retrieval would have been regarded as ridiculous even ten years ago. The rapid development of the World Wide Web has challenged all previous definitions of information access. New information sites are established almost daily, and the kinds of information available change almost as quickly. A major problem is that the information so available is no longer subject to the kinds of controls that were available in the era of books and periodicals, when information was subject to specific rules as to content and format. Libraries, therefore, have to look at other rules about accessing information. It may not always be clear what is being accessed and what are the library's rights, particularly when the provider may arbitrarily change either the content or the access software.

What Is the Meaning of Access?

Librarians now have to deal with access and downloading, as well as with purchases. The rules relating to these transactions may be very different from those relating to the traditional purchase of books and serials. Whereas purchased materials could be reused without charge to the user, accessed materials may well carry access charges as well as charges for downloading or printout. Although many librarians have already accommodated such shifts in their treatment of access to databases, they may now have to look at the same kinds of issues with regard to electronic printouts or downloadings. This may be complicated by the direction libraries have taken in providing access to electronic projects, instructional programs, or alternative information databases through their online catalog workstations, which are often now clogged by students and faculty undertaking research or preparing papers. There have always been problems with unauthorized access, for example students using the library terminals to get into central computing, but the methods available for their control are inadequate to the new setting. Even if libraries did determine to charge back all costs for access to databases and such, doing so may well be impossible, or, at the very least, so time-consuming and costly in itself as to undermine the budget even further.

Access to Information

Although it may seem unlikely that the authors and publishers of scholarly information would seek to withhold the results of their research from other researchers, the increasingly complex field of copyright and access rights seems to portend a setting within which libraries and individual scholars may find it increasingly difficult to access the information they need. The suggested solutions, such as consortial access to databases, are less than satisfactory within the total universe of information, since much information is inchoate or, at best, included in databases that are less than well defined.

Also, the internal software can often be frustrating and counterproductive, as, for example, when each new search must go back to page one, as it were, or there is no link between citation and content. There is a crying need for electronic information suppliers to work more closely with librarians in developing their products, a procedure that was only slowly and reluctantly undertaken by the publishers of printed reference works, though ultimately with great success and benefit to both parties. No research project can rely simply on one or two information sources and it is often essential to meld different kinds of information, e. g., bibliographic, textual, and numeric. The interrelatedness of specific information discoveries simply underlines the problems faced by the individual researcher and the library that is seeking to provide the appropriate information.

There is no clear way to develop library budgets to respond to the need for access to information that may well lie far outside the realm of print. In this setting, libraries, whether public, academic, or corporate, have to look carefully at their role within their governing organization.

- What are they being asked to do?
- How do they carry out that task?
- What guidelines are being supplied?
- What financial resources are being provided?

Librarians have to be wary of being dragged into situations where they are expected to provide resources and services beyond their capacity, without any assurance of the necessary financial support. This happens all too readily, because most administrators are not truly aware of the library's total needs and seem to feel that going online will eliminate all other kinds of regular library materials, which, as has been shown by the growth of interlibrary loan in response to online access, is certainly not the case.[10] Unfortunately, librarians have not managed to present their own case very well, particularly in the school setting, where it is often virtually impossible to replace out-of-date textbooks, the sort of thing that is unlikely to go online.

Contracts with the providers of database and electronic access programs do not always make clear the total extent of the library's commitment, nor do they address fully the limitations on the services provided by the originators. This leaves the librarian having to find out by experience, not usually a satisfactory way. Certainly, many vendors will arrange for instruction, and there are ongoing user groups, but the ways in which these services are provided exclude most librarians, who are unable to attend national or even regional conferences. Fortunately, many of the bibliographic library networks are taking an active role.

Summary

The rapid changes in information services have moved the library into a different financial world, where contracts and leases have joined purchase as basic ways of obtaining that information. These have very different rules both for use and for payment. There are legal issues about ownership and copyright, and librarians may often need legal instruction, just as they did when negotiating contracts for the purchase of an automated system. There are now many more players, and, in many cases, even the individual user can become a player. Libraries have to rethink their own roles within their communities, as well as recognizing that that community has itself expanded.

Notes

1. These issues were explored during the Business of Acquisitions Preconference at San Francisco in 1997, notably by Ann Okerson, who explored electronic license policy, and Trisha Davis, who explored electronic license prices.

2. Kenneth J. Bierman, "How Will Libraries Pay for Electronic Information?" *Journal of Library Administration* 15, no. 3/4 (1991): 67–84.

3. The issue of photocopy charges was addressed carefully by David Taylor in "Serials Management: Issues and Recommendations," in *Issues in Library Management: A Reader for the Professional Librarian,* ed. Adrienne Hickey (White Plains, N.Y.: Knowledge Industry Publications, 1984) pp. 82–96, where he explains that charges were inevitable if the library budget was not to be overwhelmed by the costs, and suggests that the same arguments apply to electronic access.

4. *The Economics of Information in the Networked Environment,* ed. Meredith A. Butler and Bruce R. Kingma (Washington, D.C.: Association of Research Libraries, 1996).

5. Arlene Bielefield and Lawrence Cheeseman, *Technology and Copyright Law: A Guidebook for the Library, Research, and Teaching Professions* (New York: Neal-Schuman, 1997) and their many other related publications.

6. There have been commentaries in library periodical news columns on Hawaii's extensive outsourcing program, but few of these have made any direct comparison with the much more long-standing blanket order programs. What has been missing from most of these commentaries is the discussion of what role both direct and outsourced selection can play in any library's acquisition program.

7. Murray S. Martin and Ernie Ingles, "Outsourcing in Alberta," *Bottom Line* 8, no. 4 (1995): 32–34.

8. Robert Renaud, "Learning to Compete: Competition, Outsourcing, and Academic Libraries," *Journal of Academic Librarianship* 23, no. 2 (March 1997): 85–90.

9. Betty Eddison, "Our Profession Is Changing," *Online* 21, no. 1 (January/February 1997): 5.

10. Thomas L. Kilpatrick and Barbara G. Preece, "Serial Cuts and Interlibrary Loan: Filling the Gaps," *Interlending and Document Supply* 24, no. 1 (1996): 12–20; Jody Bates Foote and Roland C. Reson, "The Unexpected Effect of Online Databases on Undergraduate Use of Interlibrary Loan," *Journal of Interlibrary Loan, Document Delivery & Information Supply* 5, no. 4 (1995): 65–72.

13

How to Develop a Resource Budget

Because the financial conditions surrounding libraries are changing so rapidly and so unpredictably, librarians have had little chance to develop new budget models to replace the existing ones based on such ratios as:

> people: library materials: operating; or,
>
> books: periodicals: other.

There have been some variations resulting from fee-based or document delivery services, but the accompanying programmatic changes have seldom been given sufficient consideration. Although there have been several studies of what is happening to the library materials budget,[1] these have not addressed the far more fundamental shift in the proportional allocation of the total library budget. In fact, limiting discussion to the library materials budget may hinder rather than facilitate any long-term changes.

Electronic access to information has brought about a major change in library finance since it has markedly increased other operating expenses, which now seem to be headed from 10 percent to 20 percent of the total budget, requiring major adjustments elsewhere since very few supporting institutions have been able to increase library budgets accordingly. This change, coupled with the corporate and governmental drive to reduce overheads (in this case most often people), has turned most previous axioms upside down. Although Jerry Campbell tried to reverse what he saw as a dangerous move away from information ownership,[2] he too failed to see how totally library budgets would be changed by the shift toward electronic information. To be fair, it must be said that his goal of expanding the library materials budget was justified and could be defended even in the electronic age, because access of any kind depends on the existence and ownership of specific publications. Even when these publications are in electronic format, the same kinds of rules for access and use apply.

Information Seeking

The information trail is often tortuous and may require the consultation of many works, both printed and electronic, before reaching the specific documents required. If these aids are not available locally, the researcher will have to find other ways of gaining access. While the local library will always need to supply as much as possible on the spot, it will find it increasingly necessary to access other collections or to provide electronic copies because the information universe is expanding exponentially while library budgets are expanding, if at all, only by a fixed percentage. The need for access to printed publications remains, particularly for materials from countries which have not yet joined the electronic universe and for the many publishers who have decided not to or are unable to provide electronic versions of their publications. While these are most likely to be small association, ethnic, or social-issue publishers, that does not in any way diminish the importance of their publications, and libraries wanting to serve their users appropriately will continue to need to pay attention to such publications from many sources and many countries. This, in turn, requires a much greater awareness of the world of print than is common nowadays and may well be a major issue in the debate over outsourcing.

The debate on electronic access tends to assume that only that kind of information is needed, ignoring the need for a much wider range of information in many social, political, and cultural areas. In another, earlier setting, this kind of exclusive approach was the reason it took African-American, Hispanic, and gay presses so long to make it into the general marketplace. Libraries would simply compound an evil if they allowed the same kind of myopia to preclude access to the wide range of electronic publications available, though they present some of the same kinds of problems, notably poor means of access, poor visibility, and problems in terms of indexing and cataloging.

Budget Redefinition

As any library sets out to redefine its budget, it has to set some priorities. While these extend across the total library budget, here we are most concerned with library materials expenditures and their equivalents. In these terms, some of the priorities are set out below.

Setting Budget Priorities

Basic Needs
>   Mission related
>   Primary community
>   Ongoing
>   One-time

Type of Material
  Monographs
  Serials
  Microforms
  Audiovisuals
  Electronic services
Special Needs
  Research related
  New programs
  Retrospective needs
  Replacements
Budgetary Settings
  Steady-state budgets
  Decreasing budgets
  Increasing budgets
  Special funds

To some extent, this is simply a restating of traditional budget divisions, but it is clear that interaction between the various subdivisions must have a major impact on traditional budget allocations, especially the tug-of-war between needs and financial capacities, given the ready ability to tap into electronic resources.

These long-established considerations need to be accompanied by other strategies relating to alternative approaches, which are suggested below. These strategies look outward to the wider information world within which the library must work to achieve its goals, and provide a kind of overlay for the earlier statement suggesting that there are alternative ways of reaching each alternative or goal.

Other Strategies
Resource sharing
Consortial agreements
Networking
Borrowing (ILL)
Document delivery
Electronic information files
Borrowing privileges
Single article purchase (in lieu of subscription)
Role definition

Together, these approaches result in the kind of alternative program approach recommended in this book, and they are suggested because they make it easier to migrate from existing budget paradigms to more adaptive methods by looking at both the nature and the uses of the information materials either purchased or accessed. Notable is the emphasis on external connections, which have not in the past been seen as part of the library materials budget. This shift leads to a more extensive consideration of the interactions between the traditional budget elements, and to seeing how these interactions affect the whole budget.

Public libraries are likely to present rather different expenditure patterns from academic libraries, since they usually include such maintenance costs as janitorial services and building upkeep. They are also likely to have a higher staff ratio, reflecting a greater expenditure on client programming, for example childrens' reading projects or adult programs relating to literacy, even though these programs may often be supported by volunteers. These differences are important in developing a transaction-based budget, because they reflect the different missions of the libraries. Moreover, because public libraries are much more clearly driven to demonstrate cost-effectiveness in the public good, they need to look closely at the ways they respond to user demand. Here, they may face the problem of defining the user benefits involved, and may have to rely more on broader social concepts than on local needs. Even here the concepts outlined by Laura Kahkonen are worth considering, since any public expenditure on library resources is usually less than would be needed to meet the same needs privately.[3]

Basic Considerations

The first need is to examine the information alternatives outlined in earlier chapters on the basis of their relationship to the library's objectives. Those objectives, at least nowadays, are likely to be financial and administrative, as well as informational. The transactional approach is not quite the same as a program budget approach, since its basis is user activities rather than library units. Some of the problems with program budgets apply here also,[4] in that it is difficult to be absolutely certain about the budgetary effects of change. Nevertheless, a conscious decision to shift from ownership to access, using whatever method, carries with it a need to reconsider the entire library budget in order to provide the needed services.

Unfortunately, this shift has not usually taken place. Rather, what has mostly been recommended so far is a changed distribution of the *library materials budget*. This is simply a surface response, since alternatives to purchasing involve staff and other support costs in somewhat different ratios from the standard purchasing procedures.[5] This approach opens the library to other kinds of problems, notably the difference between local and distance users, whether within the service area or outside. Transforming such trans- actions into an internal budget format would require an extended program for evaluating library services, such as is not currently available. There are some indications that libraries are beginning to look at these issues, but, so far, no useful financial models have emerged. This may change as further studies are conducted of distance education and the library's involvement in such programs,[6] or as public libraries adapt to the changes initiated by distant access to information.

Problems Associated with Change

One major problem is that the relative quantities of transactions to be projected, whether purchase, borrowing, or delivery, will emerge only gradually as user patterns change. In most of the experiments where the savings from serial cancellations and the like have been transferred to access programs, the money saved by cancellations has generally been used simply to pay for borrowed or "accessed" materials,[7] although there appear to be some doubts as to whether this "access" is to cancelled subscriptions or to yet other publications.[8] While it is true that this is one way of restoring to library users their access to information, it must inevitably also affect the distribution of staffing and consequently other expenditures as well. For this reason it is vital for the "new" library to look closely at information transfer alternatives and to determine the ways in which they can be financed, and to keep track of how they are used. Use statistics are thus becoming more and more important to libraries. Unless it is possible to track and record the user needs for owned or accessed materials, libraries will be unable to evaluate correctly whether their services are suitable and effective and certainly unable to determine whether there should be changes to meet either social or legal requirements.

Institutional Priorities

Any institution must decide whether it will emphasize local use, interlibrary loan, document delivery, or electronic information transfer, always recognizing that all four will continue to be necessary because of the different relationships likely between information users and information providers. The budgetary requirements of each alternative differ: staffing, for example, being heaviest in interlibrary loan, and expenditures on equipment, etc., being heaviest in electronic information transfer. Because institutional priorities differ, no general rules can be suggested, but each institution should consider carefully the role of information within its operations. For instance, public libraries should not consider that the provision of fiction is unrelated to information because numerous studies have indicated that reading is a necessary activity to sustain literacy.[9] This information should also be taken into account by academic libraries, particularly those supporting popular studies programs, given that academic libraries have tended not to collect this kind of material. The intertwining of the various library missions certainly complicates the development of adequate financial responses, but all libraries need to become more aware of such measures as justifications for their budgets. Only too often, libraries have fallen into the trap of reflecting purely local values, when their missions extend beyond the local population, since that population must reach out to others.

Alternative Models

Instead of the traditional library budget based on categories of expenditure, it has become necessary to look at transactional models. These are based principally on three alternatives.

1. Ownership based transactions
2. Access based transactions
3. Electronic information based transactions

These may also be further subdivided in terms of the kinds of response, for example circulation and in-house reading, interlibrary loan or document delivery, and local or distant databases. All these have different user conditions, and all may involve such traditional programs as reference and circulation services, although in differing proportions as they provide support in different ways. It should also be noted that even ownership-based transactions may well include not only the purchase of books and serials but also locally developed electronic media, including digitized materials. In this sense digitization is not only a technique for preservation but a form of local ownership which, however, requires a different mode of access.

Access and electronic information-based transactions, every bit as much as ownership-based transactions, require access to reference services and topical reference materials, the latter mostly in printed format (since it is highly unlikely that these kinds of publications will become electronic in any short order) to be successful. This differentiation between online and printed materials is often overlooked by the proponents of totally electronic libraries, though Clifford Lynch has warned against extravagant expectations.[10] The help provided may take the form not only of direct personal interaction in finding appropriate references but may also take the form of instruction, whether in a classroom setting or via electronic programs. In fact, instruction in the use of electronic information may well become a major library activity in the not too far distant future. Because electronic information systems change rapidly in terms of software and hardware, users need continually to adapt to the changes. Individuals are in the least advantageous position to be able to do this, and libraries need to emphasize their ability to do so.

Overheads

All library transactions carry with them various overhead costs—administration, purchase and processing of materials, equipment purchase and maintenance, space costs, and other items such as insurance and accounting. Unless these are taken into account, it is very difficult to make proper choices between transaction investments. The costs of these overheads vary widely by type and size of library system. This means that, before attempting to set up any program or transaction budget, the library must analyze carefully its existing expenditures and then attempt to project what changes would happen if it changed its mode of operation. This is certainly a very difficult future and,

FIGURE 13.1   A Functional Library Budget Scenario

Internal Support Services		External Support Services
Administration	**Owned Materials**	Bibliographic Utilities
Reference and Reader Services	In-house use	Vendors
Processing Systems	Borrowing	Consortia
	Photocopying	Associations
	Printouts	
	Downloading	
	Interlibrary Loan	
	Borrowing	
	Lending	
	Document Delivery	
	Print	
	Nonprint	
	Internal	
	External	
	Electronic Resources	
	In-house use	
	Printouts	
	Downloading	

while there are some guides available, they have seldom been developed with this kind of operation in mind. One of the most explicit models was developed in New Zealand by Coopers & Lybrand.[11] Others look at ways in which it is possible to disaggregate library activities and assign them to cost centers.[12] Even earlier studies, based on such models as PPBS (Planning, Programming, Budgeting Systems), provide insights into how to define and cost individual library programs.[13] These studies suggest ways in which libraries can assemble program costs and determine what are the most cost-effective ways of continuing in business. Some of the issues are presented in a visual format in figure 13.1. where the various programs are set out in decreasing order of dependence on local ownership, together with the needed internal and external support services. These tables suggest ways in which libraries can evaluate and prioritize their programs of service.

Change Over Time

Since all programs change proportionally with the lapse of time, whether by administrative decision or from their own internal structure, it is essential to remember that "information" budgets are *not* incremental, based on cost or price increases as were earlier library materials budgets, but on performance success, relating to the number of transactions involved. To some degree, this resembles PPBS, or simpler versions such as the one developed at Penn State in the 1970s[14] but the "programs" involved are radically different. They are no longer based on traditional library activities but rather on varieties of response to user need. This can certainly be a complex path to follow, since any specific unit within the library can be involved both directly and indirectly with any or all of the programs. If these programs are defined as owned materials, interlibrary loan, document access, and electronic access, the resulting patterns are shown in figure 13.2, which endeavors to show the ways in which each style of access impacts the library by suggesting what expenditure factors may be involved.

This kind of program organization is unlikely to stabilize over any short period of time. As new information transfer mechanisms evolve, the same kinds of changes will take place that accompanied the development and exploitation of microformats, or the evolution of cheaper or more efficient photocopy and document transmission devices. These changes can be expected to affect both library programs and their costs.

Variations can also arise from the different goals of specific libraries. While academic libraries are likely to be more concerned with specific academic programs, public libraries will need to look at different client groups. The latter will include, for example, children and young people, as well as senior citizens whose needs do not usually enter into academic library considerations. All of these will be affected by the changes in the

FIGURE 13.2 Expenditure Factors by Function

Owned Materials	Interlibrary Loan	Document Delivery	Electronic Service
Library Materials (a major cost)	*Library Materials* (a middle cost)	*Library Materials* (a minor cost)	*Databases* (a major cost)
Staff			
Management	Professional	Management	Professional
Technical services	Reference	Reference	Reference
Circulation	Circulation	Clerical	Clerical
Reserve books	Searchers	Searchers	Searchers
Collection control			
Reference			
Library instruction	Library instruction	Library instruction	Library instruction
Overheads			
Administration	Administration	(Administration?)	Administration
Systems	Systems	Systems	Systems
Maintenance	Maintenance	Maintenance	Maintenance
Equipment	Equipment	Equipment	Equipment
Communications	Communications	Communications	Communications
Cost Recovery			
Fees	Out of pocket	All costs	Out of pocket
Fines	Fee per use	(Subsidy?)	External charges
Photocopy	Photocopy		Downloading
Printouts	External charges		Printouts

Note: These factors have to be costed separately in accordance with the needs of each activity, and may vary according to the administrative determination of what is to be charged and what is to be subsidized.

information universe, and their needs will expand and change. Similarly, corporate libraries are likely to find that user needs will change in response to the kinds of information available. The implication is that library budgets will continue in a state of flux for some time to come. This situation leaves libraries with a wide area of negotiable activities, but also with a wide area of uncertainty. To some degree that uncertainty can be reduced by seeking to establish clear routes by which the library provides services.

Possible Paradigms

One of the suggestions that has surfaced, at least in the academic area, is that access and ownership will split the erstwhile serials budget, leaving the book budget relatively intact—a switch from 60:40 (serials:books) to 30:30:40 (serials:access:books)—but this leaves unanswered the problems libraries face in addressing the greatly increased amount of book and serial production.[15] Access may often mean that the user pays, and this may not be easily justified if the library has neglected to respond to a major shift in user needs.

Quite apart from the problem of having libraries decide what published items are worthy of acquisition, publishers themselves are facing increasing problems in deciding what is worth publishing and what will be purchased.[16] Librarians have to look carefully at what their acquisitions program, whether in print or online, is doing to meet user expectations. Further, unless library budgets increase to match inflation, they will be even less able to meet even minimal expectations. Electronic information is not free, whatever funding authorities may think, and will require ever-increasing expenditures. Only too many libraries, public and academic, have expanded their electronic services without taking into account other budgetary effects, and have found themselves going "into the red." This shift has a long-term effect on library budgets, whether the decision is to recover costs or not to do so. It simply aggravates the problem of dealing with library/user relations, since there are questions about individual and community benefits. Libraries will need to look ever more closely at the needs of their readers. This applies to all kinds of libraries, although it has most usually been applied to academic libraries. Public libraries, however, have to pay attention to business, industrial, and research interests in their communities, and special libraries must always be aware of where their parent companies are going.

Library-Community Relations

This suggests that libraries will need more and more to approach their user communities to determine their purchasing priorities. This may seem a truism, but in the days of approval plans and unlimited budgets, user relatedness was seldom a priority. A recent survey, reported in *Against the Grain (ATG)*, suggests that there may be a return to user-related collecting.[17] Libraries may well look carefully at the general results. These suggest for predominantly academic libraries a division of 30 percent for books, 53 percent for periodicals, and 17 percent for nonprint resources. Given the public library need to provide reading matter for children and popular materials for adults, their proportions may differ. They are also likely to spend more on visual media. On the other hand, it is important to remember that public libraries are also increasing their expenditures on electronic access, for example a doubling of their expenditures on database access. Such figures are clearly generalized and will differ according to the needs of each kind of library. If they are compared with a specific budget, the results can be enlightening and can suggest ways in which the library should proceed.

Based on representative academic library materials budgets of $100,000 and $1,000,000, divided according to the generalized expenditure ratios revealed by the *ATG* survey, and using the emerging proportions for library materials, staff, and other expenditures, the budgets shown in table 13.1 emerge. Remember that these budgets are generalized. No individual library budget need follow the exact model, but the use of these paradigms may make it easier to determine library materials expenditure and collecting objectives.

There are several caveats. These budgets do not include personnel overheads, such as retirement, health, and insurance benefits because these may be met in many different ways, not all of them related to the library's own budget. Moreover, academic budgets do not usually include such items as janitorial services or building insurance, although these may be major components of a public library budget. There will also be variations according to institutional purchasing programs, with undergraduate institutions spending more on books and less on periodicals. Moreover, in the smaller library, activities such as reference and interlibrary loan will be shared by the staff, which makes the estimation of program costs a great deal more difficult. In fact, the smaller budget assumes that the smaller staff will usually share activities, making their cost estimation that much more difficult. This is also likely to be the pattern with a small special library, which may decide that it

TABLE 13.1 Budget Proportions in Academic Libraries

TOTAL BUDGET	$332,000	$3,320,000
Books (30%)	30,000	300,000
Journals (53%)	53,000	530,000
Online resources (7%)	7,000	70,000
Electronic serials (4%)	4,000	40,000
CD-ROMs (4%)	4,000	40,000
Other electronic resources (2%)	2,000	20,000
TOTAL LIBRARY MATERIALS (30%)	100,000	1,000,000
PERSONNEL (50%)	166,000	1,660,000
OPERATING COSTS (20%)	66,000	660,000

Note: While these may simply appear to be the same budget at different financial levels, it is important to remember that what they purchase, whether people, materials, or services, will cost the same per unit in each case, so that the smaller budget has much more severe limitations. This is the reason some smaller (and special) libraries have chosen to outsource some of their operations.

is more cost-effective to outsource specific activities such as document retrieval than to spend valuable staff time on such operations, again given that special libraries are likely to be in the situation of being able to recover costs. Other kinds of libraries may not be able to follow such a pattern, unless they are allowed to charge fees or recover out-of-pocket costs.

In terms of the previous academic library materials budget these figures are, in themselves, quite startling, but they do not even begin to address the other kinds of changes that have been taking place in library budgets. Even those programs which have reassigned savings from serials cancellations to document delivery have usually failed to provide the necessary added staff. As well, any library wishing to venture into such a realm of service would do well to explore it tentatively at first, as suggested by Syring and Wolf.[18] The initial allocation can be quite low, but there should be a reserve to cover later growth and the need for added staff. Because parent institutions often regard such changes as an opportunity for reducing the total budget, librarians have to be aware of the need to explain the costs of alternative information solutions.

There is, however, the problem of inbreeding. Only the information already available will be seen as a criterion for the selection of new materials, whether printed or online, and new areas of research will only grudgingly be admitted to the collective. This has long been the pattern in academia and it is difficult to change such a mind-set. There are also questions about the role of library materials that are used by multiple disciplines. Studies at the Louisiana State University suggested, for example, that many materials in the Engineering Library were used mostly by nonengineers.[19]

In the same way, interdisciplinary research is difficult to insert into any institutional pattern, largely because its results are unpredictable. This was admitted at a discussion among chief fiscal officers during the ALA Midwinter Meeting in 1997, but there were few suggestions as to how this knowledge could be fitted into budget determination. This issue is particularly important as institutions adopt budgeting methods related to user support groups, or look at specific library outputs. The need to redefine the library's user population is growing and needs to be addressed. The basic issue is how the library should address differential user needs. The result is likely to be a somewhat diffuse network of different responses, to which no definite costs can be attached without a great deal more research.

Public libraries are likely to present rather different expenditure patterns, as shown in table 13.2. They, have, for example, to look at rather different user categories, such as children, young people, and senior citizens, as well as paying attention to such problems as poor eyesight by providing large-print collections or audiocassettes. Because they also provide such community-related services as story hours, their staff ratios are likely to be higher, even though they may also rely heavily on volunteer help. Their library materials expenditure proportions will also differ, since there will be a greater emphasis on general reading, including popular fiction, and less expenditure on expensive serials. The need to provide for children will also emphasize expenditure on printed materials, though many libraries are now finding that they have to provide terminals and electronic programs for children and young people. Similarly, many public libraries act as hosts for adults wanting to access the Internet, and this can become a very compli-

TABLE 13.2   Budget Proportions in Public Libraries

TOTAL BUDGET	$340,000	$3,400,000
Books (60%)	60,000	600,000
Journals (20%)	20,000	200,000
Online resources (5%)	5,000	50,000
Electronic serials (1%)	1,000	10,000
CD-ROMs (6%)	6,000	60,000
Other electronic resources (2%)	2,000	20,000
Audiovisuals (6%)	6,000	60,000
TOTAL LIBRARY MATERIALS (30%)	100,000	1,000,000
PERSONNEL (50%)	170,000	1,700,000
OPERATING COSTS (20%)	70,000	700,000

Note: The higher personnel costs reflect the much more direct service relationship to the user, including children and young people.

cated issue, with the possibility of charges for setting up an e-mail address and maintaining files. They are also likely to provide rooms for public meetings and may levy charges, while their budgets will certainly include janitorial and other building services, which are generally part of other budgets in academia.

Overheads

All library transactions carry with them various overheads (even if their institutions do not use this term) such as administration, purchase and processing, equipment purchase and maintenance, space costs, and other items such as insurance and accounting. Some of these were set out in figure 5.2. Unless they are taken into account it will be difficult to make proper choices between investment decisions. The costs of these overheads vary widely by type and size of library. This means that before trying to set up any program or transaction budget, the library must analyze all its existing procedures. There are some guides available, but they are seldom complete enough.[20] It is clear that libraries are in for a major budget transformation, whose results may not become totally clear for some time to come.

Relationship to Other Budget Formats

In order for both the library and its controlling authority to manage change more readily, the transactional groupings of expenditures within the library need to be reaggregated in terms of the traditional library expenditure functions and categories in order to set up an appropriate organization. Unless this transmigration is undertaken, librarians will find it increasingly difficult to manage their budgets. The existing budget has to be disassembled and reconstucted in accordance with the new direction in service terms. Disassembling a budget is easier said than done, unless there have been long-term records covering all kinds of library transactions. Librarians wishing to proceed in this direction, will have to reexamine all cost factors in the preceding years, because such operations as reference and circulation services have contributed in different ways and proportions to other activities. The resultant process is described for owned materials in figure 13.3. Similar procedures should be used for the other activities.

From this statement it is clear that deriving a transactional or functional budget, with the appropriate program costs, and then rematching it to the usual operational line-item budget is no simple task. The same was true of zero-based budgets, which led to their being discarded. This difficulty should not be seen as a reason for abandoning this kind of approach, but rather as a challenge to find ways to bring library costs and expenditures closer into line with current needs and to maintain such a linkage.

Each program carries with it a specific charge for the various library components involved and these will differ radically with the nature of the program. The fragility of such cost assignments parallels the fragility of assigning costs and benefits to any economic project. One change here, and another there, can alter the entire structure.

For this reason this kind of program organization is unlikely to be stable over any extended period of time, because new responses to need will continually emerge and will need to be incorporated within the administrative and financial structure. Lest this seem something totally new, it is worth while to remember that the same kinds of changes accompanied the development of microformats and the development of cheaper photocopy and document transmission devices. In each case, the change was heralded as a revolution,

FIGURE 13.3   Reaggregated Budgets

There is no easy way to show through a set of tables how transactional budgets can be realigned as regular, or line-item budgets, but the general principle is to separate the individual costs associated with each transaction-based program and to bring them together again according to the kind of expenditure. Thus the Owned Materials Budget would contain:

Expenditure on Library Materials, less any costs associated with other programs (the latter may be small but are not negligible).

Costs associated with processing those materials, printed or electronic.

Direct personnel expenditures for acquisition, cataloging, and providing reference assistance.

Costs associated with circulating and reshelving materials.

Costs associated with preserving those materials.

Reference service costs, other than personnel, to help patrons use the materials.

Direct costs for maintaining the collections, the systems, and the building.

Indirect costs for administrative overheads and collaborative projects.

These costs would then be integrated with similar costs from other programs.

but librarians found that they were simply added needs to be embraced by the larger concept of library service. Something similar is likely to be true of the emergence of electronic information, though it may now be on a somewhat larger scale and may require even more sophisticated responses.

Summary

The library materials budget can no longer be a separate part of the library budget because it intermingles with the objectives of all library programs. Even the allocation of library materials resources to departments or academic programs is insufficient to meet the demands of the new information age. All library transactions must be compared for cost and delivery achievement. The various budgetary lines may have to be reassembled to provide accounting control, much as had to be done with program budgets. The difference is that the concern now is less with the total cost of each program and more with its effectiveness in meeting user demand. Librarians have to look carefully at alternative information access programs and at the costs involved.

Notes

1. These studies include the following citations, but there are many more. F. R. Allen, "Materials Budgeting in the Electronic Age," *College & Research Libraries* 57 (March 1996): 133–43; Michael Buckland, "What Will Collection Developers Do?" *Information Technology and Libraries* 14, no. 3 (September 1995): 155–59; *Collection Management and Development: Issues in an Electronic Age,* ed. Peggy Johnson and Bonnie MacEwan (Chicago: American Library Association, 1994); *Collection Management for the 1990s,* ed. Joseph J. Branin (Chicago: American Library Association, 1993); *Declining Acquisition Budgets: Allocation, Collection Development, and Impact Communication,* ed. Sul H. Lee (New York: Haworth, 1993); Eileen Hitchingham, "Collection Management in Light of Electronic Publishing," *Information Technology and Libraries* 15, no. 1 (March 1996): 38–41; David S. Sullivan, "Budgeting for Users: Rethinking the Materials Budget," *The Acquisitions Librarian* 3, no. 2 (1991): 15–27.

2. Jerry D. Campbell, "Academic Library Budgets: Changing the 'Sixty-Forty' Split." *Library Administration and Management* 3 (1989): 325–33.

3. Laura Kahkonen, "What Is Your Library Worth?" *Bottom Line* 5, no. 1 (1991): 9.

4. The problem with program budgets was that they were based on the idea that the budget had to be recreated each year from scratch, whereas, in reality, almost all activities continued from year to year, and that they were very costly to implement, requiring that all activities be revalued each year. The intentions were good, but carrying them out became too onerous. None of this denigrates the real benefits of program budgets, which forced institutions to look carefully at their priorities. Zero-based budgets were even more extreme and have fallen quietly into disuse.

5. This is the kind of problem examined carefully by Michael Buckland in *Redesigning Library Services: A Manifesto* (Chicago: American Library Association, 1992) and his suggestions should be taken to heart by library budget planners. His suggestions for the future go beyond the recommendations provided in this book, but they suggest clearly the direction in which libraries will have to go if

they plan to meet their user needs in the future. He is particularly compelling in his examination of the physical space problems associated with various resource strategies.

6. One very useful publication exploring this area is *Libraries and Other Academic Support Services for Distance Learning,* edited by Carolyn A. Snyder and James W. Fox (Greenwich, Conn.: JAI Press, 1997).

7. The Scholars' Express program was developed at George Washington University and used savings from cancelled subscriptions to pay for access to and borrowing of printed versions of cancelled materials. It has subsequently been adopted by many other academic libraries, but does not address directly the issues of institutional and personal cost.

8. Based on the presentation by Chuck Hamaker at the 1996 Charleston Conference and the subsequent discussion, it is by no means clear that the subsequent requests for articles were related to the cancelled subscriptions. This lends even more strength to the move toward reducing subscriptions and increasing direct article services.

9. The connection between reading and literacy may seem self-evident, but many studies have shown that being read to and continuing to read as a child develop and maintain literacy; this facility with printed matter can only too easily be lost in adulthood unless the habit of reading persists. Television and similar visual media also rely, though to a lesser extent, on familiarity with language, and—*a major confrontation*—literacy is essential for the development and understanding of computer programs. Some of these trends are examined in studies conducted by the U.S. Department of Education and cited in the bibliography.

10. Clifford A. Lynch, "Pricing Electronic Reference Works: The Dilemma of the Mixed Library and Consumer Marketplace," in *Issues in Collection Management: Librarians, Booksellers, Publishers,* ed. Murray S. Martin (Greenwich, Conn.: JAI Press, 1995), 19–34.

11. Coopers & Lybrand, *Valuing the Economic Costs and Benefits of Libraries: A Study Prepared for the N Strategy* (Wellington: New Zealand Library & Information Association, 1996).

12. James A. Neal and Lynn Smith, "Responsibility Center Management and the University Library," *Bottom Line* 8, no. 4 (1995): 17–20.

13. Harold Chester Young, *PPBS: Planning, Programming, Budgeting Systems in Academic Libraries* (Detroit: Gale, 1976).

14. Murray S. Martin, *Budgetary Control in Academic Libraries* (Greenwich, Conn.: JAI Press, 1978), 62–74.

15. The *ATG* Annual Report survey for 1996 reported a 17 percent expenditure on nonprint resources, while three-quarters of the libraries responding reported an increase in their budget for electronic resources. *Against the Grain* 9, no. 1 (February 1997): 16.

16. *Choice* editorials: "Dollars & Sense," 34, no. 5 (January 1997): 710; "Dollars & Sense Part II," 34, no. 6 (February 1997): 902; "The Electronic Iceberg," 34, no. 8 (April 1997): 1263; "'Interesting Times' in Campus Publishing," 34, no. 9 (May 1997): 1439.

17. *ATG* survey, op. cit.

18. Millie L. Syring and Milton T. Wolf, "Collection Development and Document Delivery: Budgeting for Access," in *Advances in Collection Development and Resource Management* 2 (1996): 49–62.

19. This was mentioned by Chuck Hamaker in a presentation at the 1996 Charleston Acquisitions Conference, and confirmed by later comments from the floor.

20. There are several budget and allocation guides, many prepared by the appropriate committees of the Association for Library Collections and Technical Services (cited in the bibliography), and several standards or guidelines for library budgets, but none of these have yet adequately addressed the massive changes in the information universe.

14
Long-Term Implications

The implications of the electronic revolution are truly "revolutionary." The relationships between user, provider, and information are no longer simple. Indeed, the three categories may now intermesh regularly, affecting the eventual outcome of any transaction. While some have seen this as indicating the demise of the traditional library, the truth is much more likely to be that such an intermediary will be increasingly necessary in what is becoming an extremely complicated world. This, in turn, suggests a movement from resource-centered libraries to service-centered libraries and a consequent new emphasis on staff and operating expenses. It does not mean the demise of the traditional library collection, only that it will have to be seen within the context of a user-oriented institution.

The proponents of a totally electronic future have not always understood the many ways in which user and information interact. While it is likely that much information now in printed format will migrate to an electronic format, it is every bit as likely that printed materials will still be around. The information needs of different kinds of libraries may determine the proportions in each, but it seems likely that there will continue to be a mix. The more important change, from a service and budget point of view, is the increasing need for staff assistance. It is, for example, becoming increasingly clear that library users are sorely in need of instruction in how to use the new electronic information world. They are also looking for ways to mesh different information formats, and this need will vary greatly according to economic and social settings. Changes of this nature are most likely to affect public libraries and academic libraries serving adult and distance education; for example, community colleges. Many community college libraries have sought for a long time to offset their collection poverty, the result of budget scrimping, with innovative ways of obtaining access to information, while smaller public libraries have also had to find other ways of satisfying user needs. Sometimes this has taken the form of creative fund-raising, notably soliciting equipment and software from local companies, but that can scarcely become a standard source of income. At other times it has led libraries to cooperative programs.

Now the problem of information access is reaching into the larger academic library, where librarians can no longer pursue a policy of going it alone, but must be prepared to work closely with others, or to work out special arrangements with the major electronic providers.

Shifts in Budget Proportions

The first, and possibly the most drastic, effect on libraries will be further shifts between categories of budget expenditure. These will affect not only the library materials budget, but the personnel and supporting cost budgets. Although, for some time to come, libraries will continue to spend substantial amounts on printed and similar resources, gradually there will be a move to spend more and more on electronic materials and access. This shift will be controlled by the degree to which the publishing community moves toward electronic publication. To some extent, publishers have opted to continue with printed information until the many legal and economic issues can be resolved, but there are indications that electronic publishing will increase. This may be particularly true for what has been the academic/professional area of publishing, and certainly for newsletters and similar short-term information sources.

Accompanying this shift will be the consideration of what use costs properly belong to the library and what costs belong to the user. Whereas reading a periodical or book engendered only minimal library costs, linking up to the Internet or carrying out a search on a database add substantially to library expenditures, and will also add to vendor or publisher expenses. This dichotomy has led to the development of various fee and cost recovery processes, a development that can only be expected to gain speed in the future. Such processes have long existed in the library world, but they are now likely to be more finely honed and to reflect the new kinds of costs faced by the library. If publishers and agencies expand their cost-recovery procedures, libraries can be expected to do the same. Librarians will, however, need to pay close attention to their legal, social, and political contexts in order to determine what is or is not allowable.

Legal and Other Considerations

Librarians can provide access to owned (purchased) materials without too much thought for legal considerations, but they will have to think much more carefully about extended access to either electronic or other nonprint copyright materials. This use may involve access charges, copying charges, royalty charges, or all three. These charges differ legally, institutionally, and in terms of the user. Librarians will need to keep a constant watch on legal decisions about access to online information, since the rules surrounding its use change constantly. These reflect constantly changing perceptions about the nature and worth (or price) of information. Librarians have not had to think of these characteristics when serving their users but may now have to look more carefully at the cost relationships between publisher, intermediary, and user. Interestingly, the same scenario is being played out in the bookselling area, where the emergence of the major chains has significantly changed the relationships between publisher, bookseller, and buyer, as has been suggested by the Book Industry Study Group.[1] It is particularly interesting to find that sales to major bookstores may have skewed the best-seller list, since stores may subsequently return substantial numbers of copies of books thus listed. This calls into the question the widespread use of such lists as buying tools, but also demonstrates the key role played by people, both those making decisions about what to have available and those deciding what to read.

Library Access

If a library makes printed materials widely available, e.g., in reserve reading programs, there may be no significant individual access charges involved. The exception may be the use of several copies or offprints of articles, which may involve the payment of royalties. If the concern is with online information, the librarian may have to look at such arrangements as licensing agreements, or specific agreements for downloading. There are few guidelines in this area as yet; the best advice appears to be to ask your attorney to interpret the appropriate laws. Certainly, there will be concerns about publisher and author rights.[2] There may also be some questions about online access or downloading. Eventually, there will probably be greater costs simply for maintaining the access, even though schools and libraries have currently gained the right to access the Internet at cheaper rates, a decision that is being challenged in the courts. These changes will increase the operating costs proportion of library budgets, even if the decision is made to recover some or all costs from the user. Librarians will have to examine closely the cost-benefit ratios of the various means of access following the principles outlined by Michael Buckland.[3] Especially useful is his analysis of the necessary relationship between the document, in whatever format, and the bibliographic record. This relationship has been given far too little thought in the race to go electronic, but it is already clear that there are significant problems, which once again will affect library budgets. As Buckland says, we will need to move beyond the idea of substitution only, and look at the proper role for each kind of information providing technique. His suggestions should be taken to heart by all librarians. Because librarians have tended to think more in terms of inputs than outputs, this turnaround may be very difficult, but it is essential if they are to present their case for funding effectively. It will also provide long-term benefits from the reconsideration of programs and their reconfiguration.

Budget Proportions

The emergence of electronic information has changed forever the traditional budget proportions between books and serials, not to mention the role of reference materials. In this setting, we are looking uneasily at a balance between online and purchased materials, without any certain definition of either. The problem here is what belongs to whom? Libraries have traditionally purchased materials which were, thereafter, used by numerous borrowers. Online materials, however, occupy an uneasy position between owned and accessed materials, and cannot always be assigned to one or the other category. Librarians wishing to bring together these two modes of information access have to realize that there are difficult budget divisions to cross. These relate to the ownership of purchased materials and to the implications of access to unowned materials. The first activity is directly the responsibility of the library, controlled by it though subject to any agreements with the various suppliers, yet a setting in which the library calls the tune. The second depends, first, on the newly discovered needs of users, and, second, on the ability of the library to gain access to other collections and sources. In this case the user calls the tune, though the supplier may well provide background music.

Transactional Budgets

Transforming traditional budgets into transactional budgets would require setting up a series of transactional totals. Those in the tables presented here are generalized. Librarians desiring to undertake this kind of approach would have to reexamine their operations from this perspective. On a preliminary level some idea of the specific effects of the program approach can be gained from the many tables in *Creating a Financial Plan,* by Betty J. Turock and Andrea Podolsky.[4] It should be remembered, however, that such programs still follow the traditional library organization, though it is an essential first step in identifying specifc costs. In any event, fiscal prudence means that the old line-item budget will still have to be used for convenience in arriving at totals, and because it continues to be the most widely used financial control mechanism.

Here, we are looking at a different set of library service programs:

> Circulation and the in-house use of library materials
>
> Interlibrary loan
>
> Document delivery
>
> Database and similar electronic services
>
> Other cooperative agreements

The final category is usually minor and may actually function as an overhead cost, so it has been omitted in the scenario that follows. It is also possible that at least some kinds of reference service may stand apart, though, for the most part, they are supportive of other transactions or may form an entire such transaction, similar to the lending of a book. Deriving that cost could, however, be extremely difficult. Here, reference will be regarded as part of in-house use, since it involves use of the libraries' resources, both material and personal, though it also provides backup services for other operations. Circulation and similar activities also support interlibrary loan and document delivery. Moreover, any of these categories may be modified by decisions on cost recovery or subsidization of specific services. This decision-making process will frequently include both nonlibrarians and administrators outside the library. Figure 14.1 suggests a framework for costing out the selected programs. Clearly this required much more work than does developing a simple line-item or program budget, but the work may prove cost-saving in the long run, if only because it will be much easier to demonstrate that the library's budget needs and expenditures are based on reality.

Much more work will be required by each library in delimiting the nature and the costs of these categories to tailor them to specific situations, since their impact will vary by size and type of library. This will take a great deal of time and effort, but should eventually enable librarians to develop a better analysis of costs and benefits. Further suggestions are available from the Coopers & Lybrand study referred to earlier, which suggests ways of examining costs and benefits.[5] Other studies that provide helpful suggestions are those by Baker and Lancaster, Shuman, and Taylor.[6]

All these methods are labor intensive and require much more information about inputs and outputs than is generally available. The kinds of statistics

FIGURE 14.1 Possible Scenario for Developing a Transaction-based Budget

	Function			
	Owned Materials	**Interlibrary Loan**	**Document Delivery**	**Electronic Resources**
Activities	Circulation	Borrowing	Internal	In-house use
	In-house use	Lending	External	External sources
TOTAL				
Costs	Library materials	Library materials	Library materials	Library materials
	Staff	Staff	Staff	Staff
	Operating	Operating	Operating	Operating
	Overhead	Overhead	Overhead	Overhead[1]
TOTAL COST				
LESS COST RECOVERY				
NET COST				
TRANSACTION COST[2]				

Notes:

1. Overhead costs inlcude general administration, library systems, cooperative activities, and any other costs directed toward the library in general (specific program-directed costs should be assigned to those programs), and these should be prorated, most usually by program expenditure ratios.

2. While there is actually a transaction cost for document delivery, the intention is to recover the total library outlay (unless an element of subsidization is involved), so the library does not have to deal with this cost factor unless there is a financial failure. In that sense document delivery should be seen as outside the regular budget.

that have generally been kept in libraries are no longer adequate. Only more extensive record keeping, especially, for example, in the analysis of locally owned materials and their use, will demonstrate that the library is truly meeting its constituents' needs. In the same way it will become necessary to demonstrate that the library's users need and want electronic information services. Fortunately, such record keeping is made easier by the advent of the computer and its accompanying software.

Outsourcing

Changes in style of operation will certainly lead to changes in budgets. Principal among these is the movement toward broad outsourcing. Libraries have always cooperated with other agencies to complete some of their tasks, notably binding, but the movement now is to expand these activities to include such formerly basic library functions as cataloging. It should be noted here that this is newest for academic libraries. Public libraries have for many years used cooperatives or vendors and have used such mechanisms as the Greenaway Plan for handling multiple copies of popular materials. While there is nothing new in this kind of activity, the recent attention paid to its results in places such as Hawaii has tended to obscure both its long history and its importance to libraries. No library today could possibly internalize all ordering, cataloging, and processing, without incurring extremely high overheads. There may be some settings, for example rare and special collections, where the cost of local processing is justified, but, even there, many librarians have found it much more satisfactory to outsource specialized cataloging, for example Chinese-Japanese-Korean and similar exotic areas. Some of these issues are examined by Robert Renaud, who suggests that libraries need to learn to compete.[7] As Betty Eddison put it, "Our profession is changing" in the face of massive changes elsewhere in the world of information.[8] Change is likely to be continuous within the library world and it is important that the response be planned rather than fortuitous.

Outsourcing and similar practices can transform all library budgets. Sometimes the controlling authority would like to take back at least some of the presumed savings generated, principally in staffing but also in support expenditures, somewhat akin to corporate downsizing. The total "savings" generated by outsourcing could range from $30–40,000 in the smaller budget, to $200–300,000 in the larger budget, but remember that some of these savings would be offset by larger user services expenditures. The full impact of outsourcing requires more extensive study; witness the controversy surrounding such an endeavor in Hawaii.[9] Only further examination will clarify the good and bad points about massive outsourcing. Here the interest is in how such projects affect library budgeting. The most immediate impact is transferring staff expenditures in technical services to operating expenses. Any savings may be redirected within the library or taken back by the controlling authority. From a transactional budget point of view there are still costs associated with each transaction. Some of these issues were the subject of a panel discussion at the 1997 Spring Meeting of the New England Technical Services Librarians, where

Janet Hill expressed concerns about the continued downgrading of technical services activities. She pressed such librarians to assert the value of their contributions not only to the library but to its users, an interesting turn on Michael Buckland's point about bibliographical access. There is a difference between providing adequate service and cutting costs.[10]

Librarians, therefore, have to pay attention to the long-term effects of any decisions on both budget and service. The first derives, in large part, from the ability to deliver on the second, an effect that is often overlooked by administrators. Readers should be aware that we are now moving into an era in which service return is the most important factor in the support of public expenditures. Budgets will now need to be based firmly on output factors, rather than on input factors such as the numbers of books purchased. The evaluation of outputs is not easy, and requires much more rigorous attention to recording transactions than has usually been the case in libraries.

Financial Considerations

Given that they are now deeply involved in financial planning, it is clear that librarians will have to look closely at all transactions to determine whether they should be subject to some kind of user charge. The relationship can sometimes be settled by reference to state or local statutes, but, in many cases, librarians will be on their own to determine what course to pursue. They will also have to decide whether full or partial cost recovery is required. This is a political rather than a financial decision, though the two modes will frequently move hand in hand. Politics are an inescapable part of all administrative activities and librarians cannot afford to enclose themselves in an ivory tower.

Rethinking Budgets

Following the suggestions outlined in this book, librarians can begin to rethink the ways in which their libraries and their budgets are formulated, and find ways to encourage their sponsors to seek adequate funding, even if it is only to ensure that the textbooks available in a school library are not out of date. It is true that we are moving into an era when nonprint may assume an even greater role than print information, but the same kinds of relationship will persist, since each has a definite cost and definite kinds of limitations. Many of these are explored by Michael Buckland,[11] though even he seems to suggest that libraries will still have a high level of interest in printed materials for some time to come. But, as he points out, librarians will need to look carefully at the ways in which they can most fruitfully respond to user needs. Certainly the future will have its problems, but they can be no more difficult than those of the past. Librarians need to rethink their traditional responses, but must not discard activities and methods that have proven themselves effective, in the drive to be among the leaders in the electronic age.

As distinct from the past centuries when libraries as we know them were developing, the future will be marked by constant change, forcing the reconsideration of previous axioms. Whether we will find ourselves inhabiting virtual library space is still too uncertain to predict, but it is certain that we will need libraries that can adapt more quickly and efficiently to change than has been possible for the bricks and mortar, print-based libraries of the past. When it is possible for Princeton University to set aside more than $3 million for upgrading computers in its libraries,[12] and when national entrepreneurs agree to set aside even vaster sums of money for providing computer access to the Internet for schools and libraries, it is clear that the old times have changed and that we must be prepared to cope with a totally different financial environment. This is not to say that all the current fads are realistic or will even begin to meet future information needs, but it is certain that the next century will differ greatly from the present one. Librarians need to be prepared, not only for change, but to set up adequate defenses for their legitimate budget needs.

Funding Strategies

Librarians have not generally adopted an aggressive attitude toward their funding agencies, and such a change is probably long overdue. To some extent this requires the compilation of statistical and performance reports as suggested in this book, but it also calls for more explicit consideration of what budget elements the library needs. Unless they are willing to let libraries be relegated to unimportance, librarians will have to show much more clearly what they do and why they are important. Resource or transactional budgeting provides a way of achieving this, because it is based quite clearly on the community benefits provided by the library. Proceeding in this direction will require much more financial awareness and continual attention to budgets. While this may seem to run counter to the ethos of public service, it is essential to remember that no service is possible without adequate budgetary support.

Summary

If librarians seek simply to extend into the future their present activities, they may well find themselves considered irrelevant. Only by adapting to their own needs the strategies used by business and industry can libraries survive in a "bottom-line" age. This does not mean that librarians should adopt without thought the many current crazes that sweep through the financial world, only that they should be prepared to clean house thoughtfully and be able to present a well thought out strategy for financial survival.

Notes
   1. "Big Stores Mean Big Risks for Nation's Book Industry," *Hartford Courant* F1-2, May 30, 1997. The comments on the effects on best-seller lists were subsidiary, but an important side effect. The fragility of the nation's bookselling industry has major implications for libraries. It also reinforces the idea that neither publishers nor booksellers have very clear notions about price and value, or about how they interact. Although mentioned only briefly in the report, the problems of the smaller, specialized, or customer-oriented store resemble those of the library, which can survive only if its clientele is satisfied.

   2. Margaret Bald, "The Case of the Disappearing Author," *Serials Review* 19, no. 3 (1993): 7–14.

   3. Michael Buckland, *Redesigning Library Services: A Manifesto* (Chicago: American Library Association 1992). Several passages look at the ways in which the different media can be compared and incorporated into budget planning, and at how they fit into the concept of complete library service.

   4. Betty J. Turock and Andrea Podolsky, *Creating a Financial Plan: A How-to-Do-It Manual for Librarians* (New York: Neal-Schuman, 1992). The book includes several detailed budget projections which parallel to some extent the arguments presented here.

   5. Coopers & Lybrand, *Valuing the Economic Costs and Benefits of Libraries: A Study Prepared for the N Strategy* (Wellington: New Zealand Library and Information Association, 1996). The many tables are not easy to interpret, and any library following this method would require considerable accounting and statistical assistance.

   6. Sharon L. Baker and F. W. Lancaster, *Measurement and Evaluation of Library Services,* 2nd ed. (Arlington, Va.: Information Resources Press, 1991); Bruce A. Shuman, *The Library of the Future: Alternative Scenarios for the Information Profession* (Englewood, Colo.: Libraries Unlimited, 1989), which provides some public library scenarios; and Robert S. Taylor, *Value-Added Processes in Information Systems* (Norwood, N.J.: Ablex, 1986).

   7. Robert Renaud, "Learning to Compete: Competition, Outsourcing, and Academic Libraries," *Journal of Academic Librarianship* 23, no. 2 (March 1997): 85–90.

   8. Betty Eddison, "Our Profession Is Changing," *Online* 21, no. 1 (January/February 1997): 5. (Available as an offprint.)

   9. There have been many news references to the problems surrounding the Hawaii Public Libraries outsourcing project, but the full story has yet to be told. Outsourcing is almost as old as libraries, but the current concern appears to be with the seeming downgrading of librarians rather than with its economic benefits. What it can mean is that the notion of "the library" must extend to include all those working for it, even those who are not directly part of its staff.

  10. David Miller, "What Counts: The Value of Technical Services," *ALCTS Newsletter* 8, no. 4 (1997): 41, 44.

  11. Michael Buckland, *Redesigning Library Services*.

  12. This was mentioned at a meeting of budget and fiscal officers during the 1997 Midwinter Meeting of the American Library Association, and there were many similar statements, some of which also pointed out how difficult it was to maintain traditional expenditures, even while such extrabudget items were made available.

Selected Bibliography

Not all of the references listed here are cited directly in the text. Some are added to provide additional background or to link with other library concerns. References to news notes and similar items may not appear here.

Abel, Richard. "Information Does Not a Library Make: Three Outrageous Proposals." In *Issues in Collection Management: Librarians, Booksellers, Publishers,* ed. Murray S. Martin, 1–18. Greenwich, Conn.: JAI Press, 1995.

Access to Scholarly Information: Issues & Strategies. Ed. Sul H. Lee. Ann Arbor, Mich.: Pierian Press, 1985.

After the Electronic Revolution, Will You Be the First to Go? ed. Arnold Hirshon. Chicago: American Library Association, 1993.

Allen, F. R. "Materials Budgets in the Electronic Age: A Survey of Academic Libraries." *College & Research Libraries* 57 (March 1996): 133–43.

American Library Association. *Librarian's Guide to the New Copyright Law.* Chicago: American Library Association, 1976.

Anderson, Greg. "Complement or Contradiction: The Role of Acquisitions in the Access Versus Ownership Debate." *The Acquisitions Librarian* 3, no. 2 (#6, 1991): 3–13.

Ardis, Susan B., and Karen B. Croneis. "Document Delivery, Cost Containment, and Serial Ownership." *College & Research Library News* 48 (November 1987): 624–27.

Atkinson, Ross. "Access, Ownership, and the Future of Collection Development," in *Collection Management and Development: Issues in an Electronic Era,* ed. Peggy Johnson and Bonnie MacEwan, 92–109. Chicago: American Library Association, 1994.

———. "Crisis and Opportunity," *Journal of Academic Librarianship* 19, no. 2 (1993): 33–55.

Bailey, Charles W. Jr. "Bricks, Bytes, or Both? The Probable Impact of Scholarly Electronic Publishing on Library Space Needs." In *Information Imagineering: Meeting at the Interface,* ed. Milton T. Wolf, Pat Ensor, and Mary Augusta Thomas, 89–99. Chicago: American Library Association, 1998.

Baker, Sharon L., and F. W. Lancaster. *Measurement and Evaluation of Library Services,* 2nd ed. Arlington, Va.: Information Resources Press, 1991.

Bald, Margaret. "The Case of the Disappearing Author." *Serials Review* 19, no. 3 (1993): 7–14.

Baumol, William J., and Sue Ann Batey Blackman. "Electronics, the Cost Disease, and the Operation of Libraries." *Journal of the American Society of Information Science* 34, no. 3 (1983): 181–91.

Bennett, Scott. "Re-Engineering Scholarly Communication: Thoughts Addressed to Authors." *Journal of Scholarly Publishing* 27, no. 4 (July 1996): 185–96.

Bielefield, Arlene, and Lawrence Cheeseman. *Technology and Copyright Law: A Guidebook for the Library, Research, and Teaching Professions.* New York: Neal-Schuman, 1996.

Bierman, Kenneth J. "How Will Libraries Pay for Electronic Information?" *Journal of Library Administration* 15, no. 3/4 (1991): 67–84.

Boissonnas, Christian M. "Managing Technical Services in a Changing Environment: The Cornell Experience." *Library Resources & Technical Services* 41, no. 2 (April 1997): 147–54.

Boucher, Virginia. "Consultants for Interlibrary Loan." *The Reference Librarian,* no. 22 (1988): 233–38.

Branche, Lynne C. "Document Delivery: Where Collection Developemnt and ILL Meet: An RASD Collection Development and Evaluation Section Program." *Library Acquisitions: Practice and Theory* 18 (1994): 96–97.

Branin, Joseph A. "Managing Change in Academic Libraries." *Journal of Library Administration* 22, no. 2/3 (1996): 1–6.

Brin, Beth, and Elissa Cochran. "Access and Ownership in the Academic Environment: One Library's Progress Report." *Journal of Academic Librarianship* 20, no. 4 (September 1994): 207–12.

Bronowski, Jacob. *The Origins of Knowledge and Imagination.* New Haven: Yale University Press, 1978.

Brooks, Harley C. Jr. "The Availability of Western Series Fiction in American Libraries." *Collection Management* 17, no. 4 (1993): 49–56.

Brown, David J., comp. *Electronic Publishing and Libraries: Planning for the Impact and Growth to 2003.* New Providence, N.J.: Bowker Saur, 1996.

Brown, Linda A. "Balancing Information Needs with Serials Values and Costs." *Against the Grain* 9, no. 2 (April 1997): 22–24, 26, 28.

Buckland, Michael. *Redesigning Library Services: A Manifesto.* Chicago: American Library Association, 1992.

———. "What Will Collection Developers Do?" *Information Technology and Libraries* 14, no. 3 (September 1995): 155–59.

Budd, John M. "A Critique of Customer and Commodity." *College & Research Libraries* 58, no. 4 (July 1997): 310–21.

Campbell, Jerry D. "Academic Library Budgets: Changing the 'Sixty-Forty' Split." *Library Administration and Management* 3 (1989): 77–79.

———. "Getting Comfortable with Change: A New Budget Model for Libraries in Transition." *Library Trends* 42, no. 3 (Winter 1994): 448–59.

Campus Strategies for Libraries and Electronic Information. Ed. Caroline Arns. Bedford, Mass.: Digital Press, 1990.

Cargill, Jennifer, and Ronald D. Hay. "Achieving a Vision of a Statewide Academic Library Network." *Journal of Academic Librarianship* 19, no. 6 (January 1994): 386–87.

Carpenter, Michael. "How Can We Improve Resource Sharing? A Scholar's View." *Advances in Library Resource Sharing* 1 (1990): 59–73.

———. "If We Say Resource Sharing Is a Good Thing, Let's Mean It." *Journal of Academic Librarianship* 17, no. 4 (September 1991): 230–31.

Carrigan, Dennis P. "Commercial Journal Publishers and University Libraries: Retrospect and Prospect." *Journal of Scholarly Publishing* 27, no. 4 (July 1996): 208–21.

Chabrow, Eric R. "Copyrights." *Information Week,* no. 572 (March 25, 1996): 46–54.

Childers, Thomas A. "California's Reference Crisis." *Library Journal* 119, no. 7 (April 15, 1994): 32–35.

Chrzatowski, Tina E., and Mary A. Anthes. "Seeking the 99% Chemistry Library: Extending the Serials Collection through the Use of Decentralized Document Delivery." *Library Acquisitions: Practice and Theory* 19 (1995): 141–52.

Chrzatowski, Tina E., and Karen A. Schmidt. "Collections at Risk: Revisiting Serial Cancellations in Academic Libraries." *College & Research Libraries* 57, no. 4 (July 1996): 351–64.

———. "Surveying the Damage: Academic Library Serial Cancellations 1987–88 through 1989–90." *College & Research Libraries* 54, no. 2 (March 1993): 92–102.

Clark, Tom. "On the Cost Differences between Publishing a Book in Paper and in the Electronic Medium." *Library Resources & Technical Services* 39, no. 1 (January 1995): 23–28.

Collection Management and Development: Issues in an Electronic Era. Proceedings of the Advanced Collection Management and Development Institute, Chicago, Illinois, March 26–28, 1993. Ed. Peggy Johnson and Bonnie MacEwan. ALCTS Papers on Library Technical Services and Collections, no. 5. Chicago: American Library Association, 1994.

Collection Management for the 1990s. Ed. Joseph J. Branin. Chicago: American Library Association, 1993.

Colyer, Sue. "Effective Resource Sharing in New Zealand Libraries." *New Zealand Libraries* 47, no. 10 (June 1994): 190–93.

Coopers & Lybrand. *Valuing the Economic Costs and Benefits of Libraries: A Study Prepared for the N Strategy.* Wellington: New Zealand Library & Information Association, 1996.

"Coordinating Cooperative Collection Development: A National Perspective," ed. Wilson Luquire. *Resource Sharing and Information Networks* 2, no. 3/4 (Spring/ Summer 1985): 1–153.

Cox, Richard J. "Taking Sides on the Future of the Book." *Library Journal* 122, no. 2 (February 1997): 153–55.

Crawford, Walt, and Michael Gorman. *Future Libraries: Dreams, Madness, and Reality.* Chicago: American Library Association, 1995.

Dannelly, G. N. "Justifying Collection Budgets." *Journal of Library Administration* 19, no. 2 (1993): 75–88.

Daubert, Madeline J. *Financial Management for Small and Medium-sized Libraries.* Chicago: American Library Association, 1993.

Davenport, Tom. "Think Tank: Knowledge Roles: The CKO and Beyond." *CIO* (April 1, 1996): 24, 26.

Davis, Allan. "Database Usage and Title Analysis on a CD-ROM Workstation." *Serials Review* 19, no. 3 (1993): 85–93.

Davis, Stan, and Jim Botkin. "The Coming of Knowledge-Based Business." *Harvard Business Review* (September/October 1994): 165–70.

Declining Acquisition Budgets: Allocation, Collection Development, and Impact Communication. Ed. Sul H. Lee. New York: Haworth, 1993.

Delivery of Information and Materials between Libraries: The State of the Art. Ed. Keith Michael Fields and Ronald P. Naylor. Chicago: Association of Specialized and Cooperative Library Agencies, 1991.

Destrie, Tammy Nichelson, and Virginia Steel. *Interlibrary Loan Trends: Making Access a Reality.* SPEC Kit 184. Washington, D.C.: Association of Research Libraries, Office of Management Services, 1992.

"Dilemmas of Nonprofit Accountability." *Nonprofit Management and Leadership* 6, no. 2 (winter 1995). Special Issue.

Dreyfus, Hubert L. *What Computers Can't Do: A Critique of Artificial Reason.* New York: Harper & Row, 1972.

Drucker, Peter E. "The Age of Social Transformation." *Atlantic Monthly* 274 (November 1994): 53–80.

———. *The New Realities: In Government and Politics/ In Eeconomics and Business/ In Society and World View.* New York: Harper & Row, 1989.

———. *Technology, Management and Society.* New York: Harper & Row, 1970.

Dunn, John A. Jr., and Murray S. Martin. "The Whole Cost of Libraries." *Library Trends* 42, no. 3 (Winter 1993): 564–78.

Durkheim-Montmartin, Max E., Graf von; and others. "Library Materials Fund Allocation: A Case Study." *Journal of Academic Librarianship* 21 (January 1995): 126–32.

Eco, Umberto. *Foucault's Pendulum.* New York: Harcourt Brace Jovanovich, 1989.

———. *The Name of the Rose.* New York: Harcourt Brace Jovanovich, 1983.

The Economics of Access versus Ownership: The Costs and Benefits of Access to Scholarly Articles via Interlibrary Loan and Journal Subscriptions. Ed. Bruce R. Kingma. Co-published simultaneously in *Journal of Interlibrary Loan, Document Delivery & Information Supply* 6, no. 3 Whole issue (Binghamton, N.Y.: Haworth Press, 1996).

The Economics of Information. Ed. Jana Varlejs. Jefferson, N.C.: McFarland, 1982.

The Economics of Information in the Networked Environment. Ed. Meredith A. Butler and Bruce R. Kingsma. Washington, D.C.: Association of Research Libraries, 1996.

Eddison, Betty. "Our Profession Is Changing." *Online* 21, no. 1 (January/February 1997). Available in offprint.

"Electronic Data Interchange (EDI)": This topic is the subject of a special section in *Library Administration & Management* 10, no. 3 (summer 1996): 138–75.

Elliott, V. G. "Acquisitions and Access in Academic Libraries: The Case for Access Today." *New Zealand Libraries* 47, no. 10 (June 1994): 200–203.

Ellsworth Associates. *Study of Cities and County Library Services.* Final Report. Palo Alto, Calif.: 1991.

Erickson, Rodney. "*Choice* for Collection Development." *Library Acquisitions: Practice and Theory* 16, no. 1 (1992): 43–49.

Fairbairn, Brett. "The Present and Future of Historical Journals." *Journal of Scholarly Publishing* 27, no. 2 (January 1996): 59–74.

Fees for Library Service: Current Practice and Future Policy. Ed. Arthur Curley. New York: Neal-Schuman, 1986.

Foote, Jody Bates, and Roland C. Reson. "The Unexpected Effect of Online Databases on Undergraduate Use of Interlibrary Loan." *Journal of Interlibrary Loan, Document Delivery & Information Supply* 5, no. 4 (1995): 65–72.

Foucault, Michel. *The Archaeology of Knowledge and the Discourse on Knowledge.* New York: Pantheon, 1972.

Giacoma, Pete. *The Fee or Free Decision: Legal, Economic, Political, and Ethical Perspectives for Public Libraries.* New York: Neal-Schuman, 1989.

Goddard, Stephen B. "The Information Superhighway: Crisis & Opportunity." *Library Journal* 119, no. 12 (July 1994): 56.

Goleski, Elaine. "Learning to Say 'Yes': A Customer Service Program for Library Staff." *Library Administration & Management* 9, no. 4 (fall 1995): 211–15.

Gossen, Eleanor B., and Suzanne Irving. "Ownership versus Access and Low-Use Periodical Titles." *Library Resources & Technical Services* 39, no. 1 (January 1995): 43–52.

Gould, Stephen Jay. *An Urchin in the Storm: Essays about Books and Ideas.* New York: Norton, 1987.

Gozzi, Cynthia. "Managing Acquisitions in a Changing Environment: From Coping to Comfort." *Library Resources & Technical Services* 41, no. 2 (April 1997): 135–38.

Gross, Robert A., and Christine L. Borgman. "The Incredible Vanishing Library." *American Libraries* 26, no. 9 (1995): 900–904.

Hacken, Richard. "The RLG Conoco Study and Its Aftermath: Is Resource Sharing in Limbo?" *Journal of Academic Librarianship* 18, no. 1 (1992): 17–23.

Hardesty, Larry, and Colette Mak. "Searching for the Holy Grail: A Core Collection for Undergraduate Libraries." *Journal of Academic Librarianship* 19, no. 6 (January 1994): 362–71.

Harloe, Bart, and John M. Budd. "Collection Development and Scholarly Communication in the Era of Electronic Access." *Journal of Academic Librarianship* 20, no. 2 (May 1994): 83–87.

Harris, Thomas C. "An Interlibrary Coordination Extension Program." In *Austerity Management in Academic Libraries,* ed. John F. Harvey and Peter Spyers-Duran, 62–81. Metuchen, N.J.: Scarecrow, 1984.

Herstand, J. E. "Interlibrary Loan Cost Study and Comparison." *RQ* 20 (1981): 249–56.

Higginbotham, Barbra Buckner, and Sally Bowdoin. *Access versus Assets: A Comprehensive Guide to Resource Sharing for Academic Librarians.* Chicago: American Library Association, 1993.

Hightower, Christy, and George Soete. "The Consortium as a Learning Organization." *Journal of Academic Librarianship* 21, no. 2 (March 1995): 87–91.

Hitchingham, Eileen. "Collection Management in Light of Electronic Publishing." *Information Technology and Libraries* 15, no. 1 (March 1996): 38–41.

Holt, Glen E., Donald Elliott, and Christopher Dussold. "A Framework for Evaluating Public Investment in Urban Libraries." *Bottom Line* 9, no. 4 (1996): 4–13.

Horowitz, Irving Louis. *Communicating Ideas: The Politics of Scholarly Publishing,* 2nd expanded ed. New Brunswick, N.J.: Transaction Publishers, 1991.

Hu, Chengren, and Joyce Huang. "Toward a Model ILL and Document Delivery Automated System: A Case Study." *Journal of Interlibrary Loan, Document Delivery & Information Supply* 6, no. 4 (1996): 61–71.

Impact of Rising Costs of Serials and Monographs on Library Services and Programs. Ed. Sul H. Lee. New York: Haworth, 1989. (Also available as *Journal of Library Administration,* 10, no. 1.)

Intellectual Property and the National Information Infrastructure: The Report of the Working Group on Intellectual Property Rights. Bruce A. Lehman, Chair. Washington, D.C.: U.S. Department of Commerce, 1995.

Intner, Sheila S. *Interfaces: Relationships between Library Technical and Public Services.* Englewood, Colo.: Libraries Unlimited, 1993.

———. "Ownership or Access? A Study of Collection Development Decision Making in Libraries." *Advances in Library Administration and Organization* 12 (1991): 1–38.

———. "Stream of Consciousness: Outsourcing in Hawaii—The Next Installment." *Technicalities* 17, no. 9 (April 1997): 2–3.

Jackson, Mary E. "Integrating ILL with Document Delivery: Five Models." *Wilson Library Bulletin* (September 1993): 76–78.

James-Catalano, Cynthia N. "Library Links." *Internet World* 7 (July 1996): 32–34.

Johnson, Peggy. "Dollars and Sense," column in *Technicalities.*

Joswick, Kathleen E., and Jeanne Koekkoek Stierman. "The Core List Mirage: A Comparison of the Journals Frequently Consulted by Faculty and Students." *College & Research Libraries* 58, no. 1 (January 1997): 48–55.

Kahkonen, Laura. "What Is Your Library Worth?" *Bottom Line* 5, no. 1 (1991): 9.

Kahn, Herman, and Anthony J. Weiner. *The Year 2000: A Framework for Speculation on the Next Thirty-three Years.* New York: Macmillan, 1967.

Kane, Laura Townsend. "Access vs. Ownership: Do We Have to Make a Choice?" *College & Research Libraries* 58, no. 1 (January 1997): 59–67.

Kantor, Paul. *Levels of Output Related to Cost of Operation of Scientific and Technical Libraries: The Final Report of the LORCOST Libraries Project.* Cleveland, Ohio: Department of Systems Engineering, Case Western Reserve University, n.d.

Kaplan, David A., and Adam Rogers. "The Silicon Classroom." *Newsweek* 127 (April 22, 1996): 60–61.

Karp, Rashelle S. *The Academic Library of the 90s: An Annotated Bibliography.* Westport, Conn.: Greenwood Press, 1994.

Kemeny, John G. *Man and the Computer.* New York: Scribner, 1972. (See especially chapter 8, "Library of the Future.")

Kent, Allen, and others. *Use Study of Library Materials: The University of Pittsburgh Study.* New York: Dekker, 1979.

Khalil, Mounir. "Reaching the World through Document Delivery." In *Proceedings of the 14th National Online Meeting* (New York: Learned Communications, Inc., 1993), 233–40.

Kibirige, Harry M. *Foundations of Full Text Electronic Information Delivery Systems: Implications for Information Professionals.* New York: Neal-Schuman, 1996.

Kilpatrick, Thomas L., and Barbara G. Preece. "Serial Cuts and Interlibrary Loan: Filling the Gaps." *Interlending and Document Supply* 24, no. 1 (1996): 12–20.

Kimmel, Janice L. "ILL Staffing: A Survey of Michigan Academic Libraries." *RQ* 35, no. 2 (winter 1995): 205–16.

Kleiner, Jane P., and Charles A. Hamaker. "Libraries 2000: Transforming Libraries Using Document Delivery, Needs Assessment, and Networked Resources." *College & Research Libraries* 58, no. 4 (July 1997): 355–74.

LaGuardia, Cheryl. "Virtual Dreams Give Way to Digital Reality." *Library Journal* 120, no. 16 (October 1, 1995): 42–44.

Lanier, Don, and Kathryn Carpenter. "Enhanced Services and Resource Sharing in Support of New Academic Programs." *Journal of Academic Librarianship* 20, no. 1 (March 1994): 15–18.

Lent, Robert, Louise A. Buckley, and David Lane. "Money Talks But Can It Listen?— How We Found Out What Our Faculty Really Read." *Against the Grain* 9, no. 2 (April 1997): 1, 16, 18, 20, 34.

Libraries and Other Academic Support Services for Distance Learning. Edited by Carolyn A. Snyder and James W. Fox. Greenwich, Conn.: JAI Press, 1997.

Lougee, W. P. "Beyond Access: New Concepts, New Tensions for Collection Development in a Digital Environment." *Collection Building* 14, no. 3 (1995): 19–25.

Luther, Judy. "Full Text Journal Subscriptions: An Evolutionary Process." *Against the Grain* 9, no. 3 (June 1997): 18, 20, 22, 24.

Lynch, Clifford A. "Pricing Electronic Reference Works: The Dilemma of the Mixed Library and Consumer Marketplace." In *Issues in Collection Management: Librarians, Booksellers, Publishers,* ed. Murray S. Martin, 19–34. Greenwich, Conn.: JAI Press, 1995.

———. "Serials Management in the Age of Electronic Access." *Serials Review* 17, no. 1 (1991): 7–12.

Manoff, Marlene, and others. "The MIT Libraries Electronic Journal Project: Reports on Patron Access and Technical Processing." *Serials Review* 19, no. 3 (1993): 15–40.

Martin, James. *The Wired Society.* Englewood Cliffs, N.J.: Prentice-Hall, 1978.

Martin, Murray S. *Academic Library Budgets.* Greenwich, Conn.: JAI Press, 1993.

———. *Budgetary Control in Academic Libraries.* Greenwich, Conn.: JAI Press, 1978.

———. "Buying, Borrowing, and Bibliographers: Some Observations on Collection Development Flexibility." *Library Acquisitions: Practice and Theory* 3 (1979): 115–22.

———. *Collection Management and Finance: A Guide to Strategic Library Materials Budgeting.* Chicago: American Library Association, 1995.

———. "Cost Containment and Serial Cancellation." *Serials Review* 18, no. 3 (1992): 64–65.

———. "Fiscal Currents," column in *The Bottom Line.*

———. "Interlibrary Loan and Document Delivery: Costs and Fees." *Bottom Line* 9, no. 4 (1996): 27–31.

———. "The Invasion of the Library Materials Budget by Technology. Serials and Databases: Buying More with Less?" *Serials Review* 18, no. 3 (1992): 7–17.

———. "Is Your Library Reference Poor?" *Technicalities* 16, no. 1 (January 1996): 5–7, and 16, no. 2 (February 1996): 1, 5–7.

———. "Money Matters," column in *Technicalities*.

———, and Ernie Ingles. "Outsourcing in Alberta." *Bottom Line* 8, no. 4 (1995): 32–34.

———, and Paul Kobulnicky. "The Role of the Library in Institutional Development." *Bottom Line* 9, no. 1 (1996): 40–42.

———, and Betsy Park. *Setting Fees and Fines: A How-to-Do-It Manual for Librarians.* New York: Neal-Schuman, 1998.

Mason, Marilyn Gell. "The Future Revisited." *Library Journal* 121, no. 12 (July 1996): 70–72.

McCombs, Gillian M. "Notes on Operations: The Internet and Technical Services: A Point Break Approach." *Library Resources & Technical Services* 38, no. 2 (April 1994): 169–77.

McLuhan, Marshall. *Understanding Media: The Extensions of Man.* New York: McGraw-Hill, 1964.

Meadow, Charles T. "On the Future of the Book, or Does It Have a Future?" *Journal of Scholarly Publishing* 26, no. 4 (July 1995): 187–96.

Meadows, Jack, David Bullinger, and Peter Such. "The Cost of Implementing an Electronic Journal." *Journal of Scholarly Publishing* 26, no. 4 (July 1995): 167–73.

Mellendorf, Scott A. "Pounding the Pavement with Purpose: Utilizing the Information Superhighway for Daily Work Tasks." *RQ* 35, no. 2 (winter 1995): 231–35.

Melville, Annette. *Resource Strategies in the 90s: Trends in ARL University Libraries.* Occasional Paper no. 16. Washington, D.C.: Association of Research Libraries, Office of Management Services, 1994.

Metz, Paul. "Thirteen Steps to Avoiding Bad Luck in a Serials Cancellation Project." *Journal of Academic Librarianship* 18, no. 2 (1992): 76–82.

Mielke, Linda. "Short-range Planning for Turbulent Times." *American Libraries* 26, no. 9 (1995): 905–6.

Mitchell, Eleanor, and Sheila A. Walters. *Document Delivery Services: Issues and Answers.* Medford, N.J.: Learned Information Inc., 1995.

Naisbitt, John, and Patricia Aburdene. *Megatrends 2000: Ten New Directions for the 1990s.* New York: Morrow, 1990.

Neal, James G. "Academic Libraries: 2000 and Beyond." *Library Journal* 121, no. 12 (July 1996): 74–76.

———, and Lynn Smith. "Responsibility Center Management and the University Library." *Bottom Line* 8, no. 4 (1995): 17–20.

New Zealand Library and Information Association. Joint Standing Committee on Interloan. *Revised Proposal for a New Model for Inter-Library Loan in New Zealand.* Wellington: NZLIA, 1996.

Nielsen, Brian. "Allocating Costs, Thinking about Values: The Fee-or-Free Debate Revisited." *Journal of Academic Librarianship* 15 (1989): 211–17.

Niemeyer, M., and others. "Balancing Out the Library Materials Budgets." *Technical Services Quarterly* 11, no. 1 (1993): 43–60.

Pederson, Wayne, and David Gregory. "Interlibrary Loan and Commercial Document Supply: Finding the Right Fit." *Journal of Academic Librarianship* 20, no. 5/6 (November 1994): 263–72.

Penzias, Arno. *Ideas and Information: Managing in a High-Tech World.* New York: Norton, 1989.

Perrault, Anna H. "The Changing Print Resource Base of Academic Libraries in the United States." *Journal of Education for Library and Information Science* 36, no. 4 (fall 1995): 295–308.

Price, Anna L., and Kjestine R. Carey. "Serials Use Study Raises Questions about Cooperative Ventures." *Serials Review* 19, no. 3 (1993): 79–84.

Public Library Association. Public Policy for Public Libraries Section. Fee-Based Services Committee. *Position Paper on Fee-Based Services.* Chicago: PLA, 1996.

Quinn, James Brian, Philip Anderson, and Sydney Finkelstein. "Managing Professional Intellect: Making the Most of the Best." *Harvard Business Review* (March/April 1996): 71–80.

Renaud, Robert. "Learning to Compete: Competition, Outsourcing, and Academic Libraries." *Journal of Academic Librarianship* 23, no. 2 (March 1997): 85–90.

Resource Sharing and Information Networks 7, no. 1 (1991), whole issue devoted to cooperation.

Risher, Carol A., and Laura N. Gasaway. "The Great Copyright Debate." *Library Journal* 119, no. 15 (September 15, 1994): 34–37.

Roberts, Elizabeth P. "ILL/Document Delivery as an Alternative to Local Owneership of Seldom-Used Scientific Journals." *Journal of Academic Librarianship* 18, no. 1 (1992): 30–34.

Roche, Marilyn M. *ARL/RLG Interlibrary Loan Cost Study: A Joint Effort by the Association of Research Libraries and the Research Libraries Group.* Washington, D.C.: ARL, 1993.

Rottman, F. K. "To Buy or Borrow: Studies of the Impact of Interlibrary Loan on Collection Development in the Academic Library." *Journal of Interlibrary Loan & Information Supply* 1, no. 3 (1991): 17–27.

St. Lifer, Evan. "Public Library Budgets Brace for Internet Costs." *Library Journal* 122, no. 1 (January 1997): 44–47.

Schaffner, Ann C., Marianne Burke, and Jutta Reed-Scott. "Automated Collection Analysis: The Boston Library Consortium Experience." *Advances in Library Resource Sharing* 3 (1992): 35–49.

Schement, Jorge Reina. "A 21st-Century Strategy for Librarians." *Library Journal* 121, no. 8 (May 1, 1996): 34–36.

Schockmel, R. B. "The Premise of Copyright: Assaulting on Fair Use and Royalty Use Fees." *Journal of Academic Librarianship* 22 (January 1996): 15–25.

Scholarly Communication in an Electronic Environment: Issues for Research Libraries. Ed. Robert Sidney Martin. Chicago: Association of College and Research Libraries, 1993.

Seaman, Scott. "Impact of Basic Books vs. Kinko's Graphics on Reserve Services at the University of Colorado, Boulder." *Journal of Interlibrary Loan, Document Delivery and Information Supply* 5, no. 3 (1995): 111–16.

Shuman, Bruce A. *The Library of the Future: Alternative Scenarios for the Information Profession.* Englewood, Colo.: Libraries Unlimited, 1989.

Sievers, Arlene Moore. "Books in Limbo: Book Distribution and Supply Problems That Affect Academic Libraries." In *Issues in Collection Management: Librarians, Booksellers, Publishers,* ed. Murray S. Martin, 129–42. Greenwich, Conn.: JAI Press, 1995.

Simmons, R., and G. Hanks. "Equitable Non-Resident Fees Are Critical in the Provision of Library Services for All Idahoans." *Idaho Librarian* 47 (July 1995): 82.

Steele, Victoria, and Stephen D. Elder. *Becoming a Fundraiser: The Principles and Practice of Library Development.* Chicago: American Library Association, 1992.

Sullivan, David S. "Budgeting for Users: Rethinking the Materials Budget." *The Acquisitions Librarian* 3, no. 2 (1991): 15–27.

Syring, Millie L., and Milton T. Wolf. "Collection Development and Document Delivery: Budgeting for Access." *Advances in Collection Development and Resource Management* 2 (1996): 49–62.

Taylor, Arlene G. "The Information Universe: Will We Have Chaos or Control?" *American Libraries* 25, no. 7 (July/August 1994): 629–32.

Taylor, David C. "Serials Management: Issues and Recommendations." In *Issues in Library Management: A Reader for the Professional Librarian,* ed. Adrienne Hickey, 82–96. White Plains, N.Y.: Knowledge Industry Publications, 1984.

Taylor, Robert S. *Value-Added Processes in Information Systems.* Norwood, N.J.: Ablex, 1986.

Thinking Robots, an Aware Internet, and Cyberpunk Librarians. Ed. R. Bruce Miller and Milton T. Wolf. Chicago: Library and Information Technology Association, 1992.

Tilson, Yvette. "Income Generation and Pricing in Libraries." *Bottom Line: Managing Library Finances* 8, no. 2 (1995): 23–36.

Toffler, Alvin. *The Third Wave.* New York: Morrow, 1980.

———, and Heidi Toffler. *Creating a New Civilization: Politics of the Third Wave.* Atlanta: Turner, 1994.

Truesdell, Cheryl B. "Is Access a Viable Alternative to Ownership? A Review of Access Performance." *Journal of Academic Librarianship* 20, no. 4 (September 1994): 200–206.

Turock, Betty J., and Andrea Podolsky. *Creating a Financial Plan: A How-to-Do-It Manual for Librarians.* New York: Neal-Schuman, 1992.

U.S. Department of Education. National Center for Education Statistics. *Executive Summary of the NAEP 1992 Reading Report Card for the Nation and the States.* Washington, D.C., 1993.

———. *NAEP Trends in Academic Progress: Science, Mathematics, Reading, Writing.* Washington, D.C., 1993.

Valauskas, Edward J., and Nancy R. John. *Internet Initiative: Libraries Providing Internet Services and How They Plan, Pay, and Manage.* Chicago: American Library Association, 1995.

Van House, Nancy A., Beth T. Weil, and Charles R. McClure. *Measuring Academic Library Performance: A Practical Approach.* Chicago: American Library Association, 1990.

Ward, Suzanne M. *Starting and Managing Fee-Based Information Services in Academic Libraries.* Greenwich, Conn.: JAI Press, 1997.

Warner, Alice Size. *Making Money: Fees for Library Services.* New York: Neal-Schuman, 1989.

Weaver-Meyers, Pat, Shelley Clement, and Carolyn Mahin. *Interlibrary Loan in Academic and Research Libraries: Workload and Staffing.* Washington, D.C.: Association of Research Libraries, Office of Management Services, 1988.

———, and Yem Fong. "Interlibrary Loan and Document Delivery: The Debate over Union Lists." *Library Administration & Management* 9, no. 4 (1995): 204–6.

Webster, Duane, and Mary E. Jackson. "Key Issue: The Peril and Promise of Access." *Journal of Academic Librarianship* 20, no. 5/6 (November 1994): 261–62.

Webster, Judy D. "Allocating Library Acquisition Budgets." *Journal of Library Administration* 19, no. 2 (1993): 57–74.

Whalen, E. L. *Responsibility Center Budgeting*. Bloomington: Indiana University Press, 1991.

White, Herbert S. "Cost-Effectiveness and Cost-Benefit Determinations in Special Libraries." *Special Libraries* 70, no. 4 (April 1978): 163–69.

Whitson, William L. "The Way I See It: Free, Fee, or Subsidy: The Future Role of Libraries." *College & Research Libraries News* 55, no. 7 (July–August 1994): 426–27.

Wiemers, Eugene L. "Financial Issues for Collection Managers in the 1990s." In *Collection Management and Development,* ed. Peggy Johnson and Bonnie MacEwan, 111–20. Chicago: American Library Association, 1994.

Wiesner, Margot. "The Impact of EDI on the Acquisitions Process." *Library Archives & Management* 10, no. 3 (summer 1996): 155–60.

Woodsworth, Anne, and J. F. Williams II. *Managing the Economics of Owning, Leasing, and Contracting Out Information Services*. Brookfield, Vt.: Ashgate, 1993.

Wooliscroft, Michael. "Access and Ownership: Academic Libraries, Collecting and Service Responsibilities, and the Emerging Benefits of Electronic Publishing and Document Supply." *New Zealand Libraries* 47, no. 9 (March 1994): 170–80.

Young, Arthur P., and Thomas A. Peters. "Reinventing Alexandria: Managing Change in the Electronic Library." *Journal of Library Administration* 22, no. 2/3 (1996): 21–41.

Zappen, Susan H. "From Cancellation to Collaboration—Some Thoughts." *Against the Grain* 9, no. 3 (June 1997): 1, 16, 68+.

Index

Murray S. Martin was born and educated in New Zealand, with degrees in English, accounting, and library science. He has worked in academic and special libraries in New Zealand, Canada, and the United States, in both acquisitions and administration, and has taught courses in English and comparative literature as well as collection development. He retired from Tufts University after nine years, as University Librarian and Professor of Library Science Emeritus, and continues to write, consult, and speak on library topics. He has a special interest in library finance and collection management. His recent books include *Academic Library Budgets,* (JAI Press, 1993), *Collection Management and Finance: A Guide to Strategic Library Materials Budgeting* (American Library Association, 1995), and *Assessing Fees and Fines* (Neal-Schuman, 1997). He has been active in several library associations. He currently contributes financial columns to *Technicalities* and *The Bottom Line.* In retirement, he has had more time to devote to his other lifetime interest, Commonwealth literature, and has also given papers and written articles in this field.

Milton T. Wolf is Vice President for Collection Programs at the Center for Research Libraries. He is also both a scholar and teacher of science fiction. He was founding editor of *Technicalities,* coeditor of *Thinking Robots, an Aware Internet, and Cyberpunk Librarians,* of a special issue on "The Information Future" in *Information Technology and Libraries,* of the 1996 science fiction anthology *Visions of Wonder* (New York: Tor), and editor of a 1997 special issue of *Shaw: Shaw and Science Fiction* (Penn State University Press).